insight text guide

Scott Hurley

I Am Malala

Malala Yousafzai
with Christina Lamb

First published in 2019, reprinted in 2022, 2023.

Insight Publications Pty Ltd
3/350 Charman Road
Cheltenham VIC 3192
Australia
Tel: +61 3 8571 4950
Fax: +61 3 8571 0257
Email: books@insightpublications.com.au

www.insightpublications.com.au

A catalogue record for this book is available from the National Library of Australia

Malala Yousafzai and Christina Lamb's I Am Malala / Scott Hurley

ISBNs:
9781925778519 (print)
9781925778526 (digital)
9781925778533 (bundle: print + digital)

Cover design by Gisela Beer, based on a concept by The Modern Art Production Group

Printed by Markono Print Media Pte Ltd

contents

CHARACTER MAP

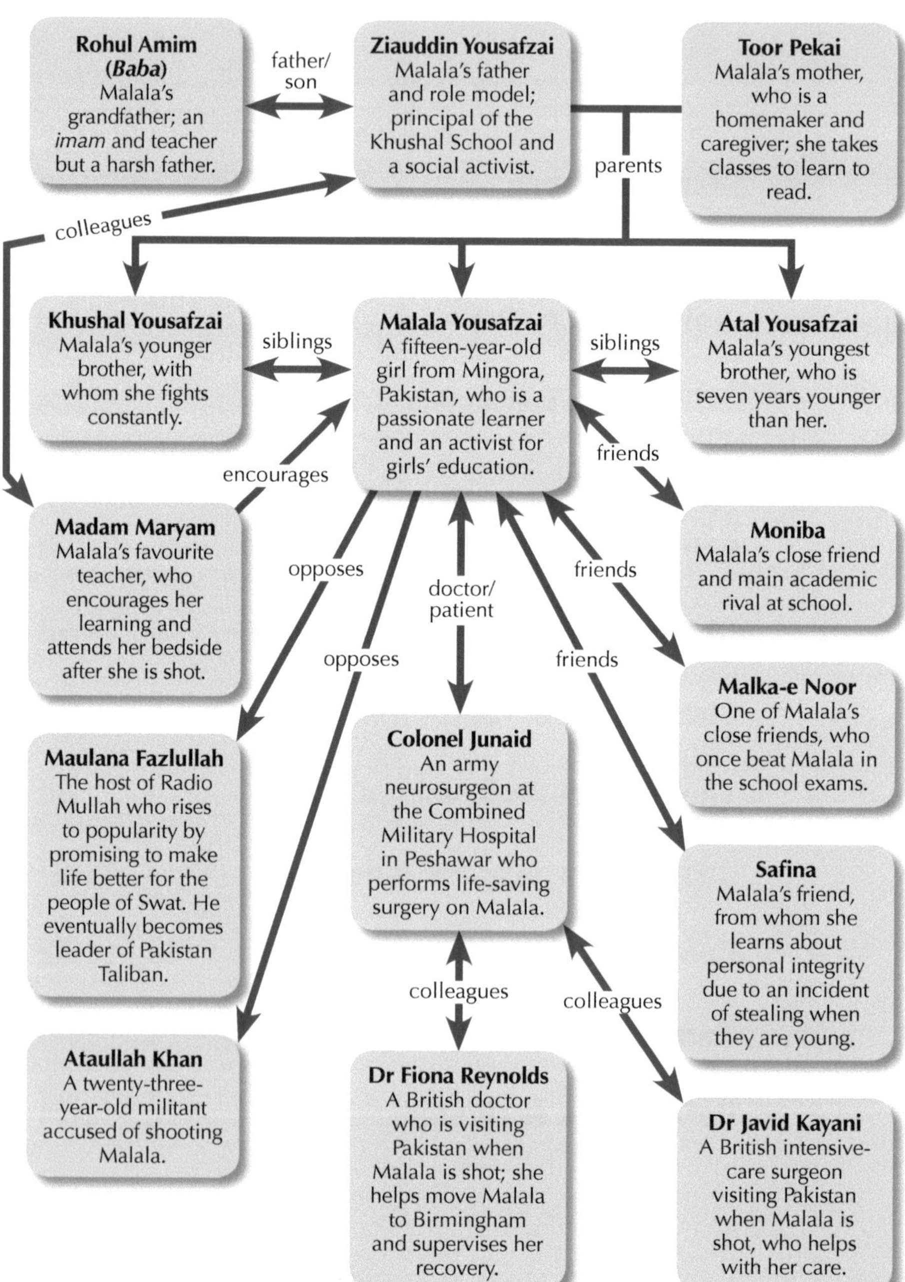

OVERVIEW

About the authors

Malala Yousafzai was born in 1997 to a Pashtun family in Mingora, the largest town of the Swat Valley in northwest Pakistan. She came to international attention in her early teens as an activist for girls' rights to education. The Taliban, with the covert cooperation of the Pakistani military, increased their influence over the Swat Valley between 2007 and 2009. Among other oppressive measures they put a stop to education for girls. Malala's father, Ziauddin Yousafzai, the owner and principal of her school, was also outspoken against the Taliban and their military protectors. Both Malala and Ziauddin were threatened with murder, and Malala was shot in the head on 9 October 2012. Following an international outcry, she was flown to Birmingham, England for treatment. Her family joined her and settled there, deeming it too dangerous to return to Pakistan. Malala made a full recovery. In 2014 she was awarded the Nobel Peace Prize along with Kailash Satyarthi, an Indian activist for children's rights. She has founded a charitable organisation, the Malala Fund, dedicated to providing education for children around the world. She has also spoken out on such issues as the persecution of the Rohingya people of Myanmar, and on behalf of children displaced by the Syrian civil war. Malala resumed her schooling in Birmingham and in 2017 began her tertiary studies at Oxford University.

Christina Lamb is an award-winning foreign correspondent and a writer of nonfiction books. She began her journalism career covering the Soviet occupation of Afghanistan and has reported from that country ever since. She has also covered Pakistan extensively, including reports on connections between the ISI (Inter-Services Intelligence, the Pakistani intelligence agency) and the Taliban.

Synopsis

I Am Malala begins with the attempted assassination of Malala Yousafzai. It then turns to the beginning of her life, interspersing stories of her early upbringing with others about her parents' lives before her birth. Both her father, Ziauddin, and her mother, Toor Pekai, were born into poverty. We follow her father's struggles to acquire an education and later fulfil his dream of opening a school. The book goes into great depth about the political history of Pakistan and of the Pashtun people, the ethnic group to which Malala's family belongs. This information is presented along with the biographies of her parents and the 'story' of Malala herself.

As she grows older, the narrative focuses on Malala: on her early years, her relationships with friends and members of her extended family, and her schooling. This last category comes to the fore when the Taliban enter the Swat Valley and begin threatening educators like her father. Malala describes in detail the atrocities committed against those whom the Taliban label 'bad' Muslims. Yet many of the Pashtuns of the valley embrace the Taliban, seeing them as protectors of traditional ways threatened by the Punjabi-controlled Pakistani government and by the US-led coalition fighting the Taliban in neighbouring Afghanistan. These Pashtuns seem to accept the assertions of their leader, Maulana Fazlullah, that the devastating earthquake of 2005 was a result of the sinful behaviour of the people.

Malala writes about her strong desire to be educated, including her competitiveness at school with her best friend, Moniba, and her academic rival, Malka-e-Noor, and her anxieties about taking tests. Only when the Taliban threaten to take away her right to go to school does she realise how vitally important education is. Ziauddin speaks out against the Taliban from the start, but Malala's mother initially finds their message of total devotion to Islam appealing. Toor Pekai turns against the Taliban when they place further restrictions on the few rights women have in Pashtun society, and on education.

Much of the narrative is devoted to the activities of Ziauddin. As his school grows in size, he joins many associations, such as the Swat Council of Elders, and gains influence in the community. He uses every forum to speak against the Taliban. As he is often away from home, the burden of raising Malala and her two brothers (and the numerous relatives and poor students the family takes in) falls to Toor Pekai.

Once the Taliban officially ban girls from attending schools, Malala begins writing a blog for the BBC under the alias Gul Makai. She also becomes the subject of a short video broadcast on the *New York Times* website, bringing international exposure. The Pakistani military occupies the Swat Valley but soon reaches a truce with the Taliban. This only emboldens the group to step up their killings and the destruction of schools. When the military comes back in force for a serious battle, the family flees, along with many other residents. After the valley is ostensibly cleared of the Taliban, the residents return, but soon disastrous floods strike the country. The Taliban, who were never completely cleared out by the army, start staging random attacks around Pakistan. Malala keeps up her activism, winning awards and giving many interviews. Soon it becomes apparent that Malala and Ziauddin are on a Taliban death list.

The narrative slows down on the day of the assassination attempt, and Malala's treatment and evacuation to Birmingham are recounted in great detail. After many logistical complications, the family is reunited with her in England ten days after the attack. The book ends ten months later, having looked at some of the effects of displacement on different members of the family. Though in exile, Malala is reinspired by her survival to dedicate her life to the rights of children to education.

Character summaries

Malala

The central figure in this memoir, Malala comes under threat from the Taliban but does not cease her activism for girls' rights to education. She is shot but recovers and ends the book living in exile in the United Kingdom. *I Am Malala* covers more than her activism; it takes great pains to portray her as a 'normal' Pashtun girl: obedient to her father, deeply religious, yet subject to the same interests and rivalries as any teenager. She is passionate about education and enjoys politics, the murdered former Prime Minister Benazir Bhutto being one of her idols; Malala hopes to return one day to Pakistan, perhaps as a politician.

Ziauddin

Malala's father is an idealistic and energetic campaigner for education and the environment. He opens a school after much struggle and nurtures it into a success. When the Taliban come to Swat he bravely campaigns against them at every opportunity. His activities frequently take him away from home, and the family constantly worries about his safety.

Toor Pekai

Malala's mother is a devout Muslim and strictly follows the rules of purdah (the veiling of women). Although uneducated and illiterate, she is a strong influence on the family, in charge of the domestic sphere – including the many relatives and acquaintances who live in their house. Ziauddin's absences also require her to undertake tasks usually restricted to men. She worries about Malala's exposure to harm, through her activism, but does not try to stop her.

Khushal and Atal

Khushal and Atal are Malala's little brothers. She and Khushal, who are close in age, fight frequently, but she gets along well enough with the much younger Atal.

Hidayatullah

Ziauddin's partner in the first school they opened goes on to work for the Pakistani government. He remains friends with Ziauddin and becomes an important conduit of information and advice for the family later when Ziauddin and Malala are threatened by the Taliban.

Moniba

Moniba is Malala's best friend. The two girls do everything together and though they often fight they invariably make up. Bright and ambitious like Malala, Moniba is always worried that her four brothers might pull her out of school. She provides an example of the kinds of limitations Malala might have faced had she not been encouraged and supported in her activism by Ziauddin.

Baba

Ziauddin's father, Malala's *baba* (grandfather) dominates the story of Ziauddin's early life. A strict man who tormented his son for his stutter, *Baba* nevertheless gives Ziauddin something the latter considers to be the most important thing in the world: a good education.

Dr Fiona Reynolds and Dr Javid Kayani

Two doctors from Birmingham, Dr Fiona and Dr Javid happen to be in Pakistan on the day that Malala is shot; without their intervention she might have died. After international outcry, Malala is evacuated from Pakistan for better treatment. The doctors' presence helps persuade the authorities to send her to Birmingham, where Malala and her family have since made their home.

Maulana Fazlullah

The leader of the Taliban in the Swat Valley, Fazlullah was a high-school dropout and operator of a conveyance for crossing the Swat River. His charismatic radio broadcasts pave the way for the Taliban takeover, winning over many Pashtuns to his inflexible interpretations of Islam. As a leader he proves oppressive and bloodthirsty.

BACKGROUND & CONTEXT

Pakistan

Pakistan became an independent nation in 1947 after the partitioning of the former British colony of India into a Hindu-dominated country (modern India) and a smaller Muslim-dominated one (Pakistan). In 1971, East Pakistan broke away to become the nation of Bangladesh. Originally envisioned as a secular democracy by its founder, Mohammad Ali Jinnah, Pakistan has endured a number of military-led governments and its civilian governments have increasingly depended on approval from the nation's dominant Sunni institutions.

The period of partition in 1947 saw the chaotic movement of tens of millions of people across the new border – Muslims fleeing India for Pakistan and Hindus fleeing in the opposite direction. Some two million people were killed in violent eruptions in this period, Malala's grandfather nearly being one of them (p.75). There has been bitter animosity between the nations ever since, and each has had nuclear weapons since the late 1990s. Though Pakistan is a large nation by world standards, its rival's population is larger by more than a billion people.

In addition to Jinnah, Malala's other Pakistani political idol is former Prime Minister Benazir Bhutto. Unfortunately for Pakistan, the regimes of democratically elected leaders tend to be bookended by much longer military dictatorships. Benazir's father, Prime Minister Zulfikar Ali Bhutto, was executed by General Zia after a coup in 1977, and Benazir herself succeeded Zia after his death in a suspicious air crash (1988). In 2007, months after returning to Pakistan following years in exile, Benazir was assassinated by fundamentalists; this happened during the rule of Pervez Musharraf, another general who had taken charge of the country by force.

Zia was the man most responsible for allowing fundamentalist Islam to become a political force in Pakistan. (This period is covered in some detail in *I Am Malala*, pp.23–6). When the Soviet Union invaded neighbouring Afghanistan in 1979, Pakistan became indispensable to the United States' campaign to undercut the Soviets. Violent fundamentalism became a tool to organise and encourage tens of thousands of men from around the Islamic world to fight in Afghanistan. The US armed them, trained them, and financed organisations devoted to turning them into jihadis (warriors for Islam). Malala's father refers to the '"Arabisation" of Pakistan' in this period (p.80). Pakistan is not an Arab country, but during the Cold War in the 1980s radicalisation in education and religious indoctrination (characteristic of nations like Saudi Arabia) exploded; this was mostly achieved through a network of *madrasas* (Islamic schools) funded by the US and its Arab allies. Many students were the orphaned boys of jihadis.

Once the Soviets were gone from Afghanistan (1989), many of these trained, armed and radicalised men, usually referred to as *mujahideen*, turned against their Western benefactors. Thus, ironically, the United States' Cold War ploy in Afghanistan was midwife to the Taliban, al-Qaeda and numerous other terrorist organisations founded by *mujahideen*. The twenty-first-century 'War on Terror' has been waged against these organisations for nearly two decades now at the cost of hundreds of thousands of lives, millions of refugees and trillions of dollars.

Like General Zia before him, Musharraf was transformed overnight from pariah (outcast) to ally with the US invasion of Afghanistan in late 2001. (This history forms a background to Malala's life in Pakistan, and is covered in depth in Chapters 5–7, 10 and 14.) Musharraf would eventually be removed in 2008 under threat of impeachment; his rule has been succeeded by a series of less powerful civilian governments.

Its history demonstrates that real power in Pakistan lies with the military. Always afraid of being crushed by its stronger neighbours (not just India, but China and, until 1991, the Soviet Union) Pakistanis have sheltered under a siege mentality and supported a strong military, making a tacit bargain to let it have free reign. The nation sees itself as a fortress of Islam. The ISI, nominally under the control of the prime minister, is actually nested within the military and is extremely powerful. It was instrumental in organising the Afghan *mujahideen*, creating the Taliban in Afghanistan and financing and protecting the Taliban in Pakistan. It would be difficult, if not impossible, for a civilian government in Pakistan to survive without the support of the military and, by extension, the ISI.

Pashtuns

The Yousafzais belong to a large Pashtun tribe. Pashtuns speak Pashto and originate in Afghanistan; they occupy the mountainous area straddling Afghanistan and Pakistan. (Pashtuns have also been known by their Hindu name, Pathans.) There is a strong Pashtun tradition of two-line poetry, called *tapey* (plural; singular *tapa*). One *tapa* evoked several times in *I Am Malala* states that the Pashtun attachment to homeland is so strong that they will only ever leave it because of love or poverty. Of the forty million Pashtuns, Malala tells us, ten million have had to leave because of poverty (p.51).

Perhaps the most conservative of Pakistan's many ethnic groups, Pashtuns live by a code called *Pashtunwali*, which compels them to offer hospitality to anyone who demands it (Ziauddin loses his first business partner due to financial pressures when relatives descend on him for food and shelter as soon as he opens his first school). Honour is paramount; the Pashtuns are sometimes a belligerent people, and some of the worst feuds happen among extended families. An insult must be paid for with the blood of a male member of the family of the guilty person (see the story of Sher Zaman, p.60). Pashtuns are known to close ranks when threatened by outsiders, yet – the authors of this text write – they are remarkably subservient to leaders, even those installed by the Pakistani capital Islamabad (p.62).

Of most importance to *I Am Malala* are the oppressive limitations *Pashtunwali* places on women. Girls as young as ten are sold into marriage by their fathers or given as wives to patch up feuds between families, without having any say in the matter. Widows are denied the right to marry again without the permission of a male family member, and girls can be killed by their family, without reprisal, simply for flirting with boys (pp.54–5). Most Pashtun women are never taught to read or write. Once they reach puberty, their lives are essentially limited to the home. They are not allowed to leave the house without a male family member, of whatever age, to accompany them. It is considered an insult to a man to be accused of consulting with his wife, as Ziauddin does with Toor Pekai (p.17). Women are kept from many occupations and are not allowed to attend mosque.

The Taliban

The Taliban formed in the mid-1990s during the long civil war in Afghanistan after the Soviet pull-out in 1989. *Taliban* is a Pashto word meaning 'students'. The group was founded with the intention of imposing strict sharia law (religious law of Islam) and purifying Afghan society. Though the organisation attracted fighters from outside Afghanistan and Pakistan, most Taliban members are, like its founders, Pashtuns; the Taliban's social program has its foundation in the *Pashtunwali* code, albeit taken to extremes. The Pakistani *madrasas* supplied large numbers of Taliban fighters: young men detached from family and tribal connections. They were educated exclusively in a particular interpretation of Islam and kept completely apart from females – whom they were taught to view as so inferior as to be almost inhuman.

The Taliban became the dominant force in Afghanistan in the late 1990s (though never gaining control over the entire country). They came to international attention for barbaric public displays of punishment – whippings and executions, including beheadings in stadiums with local people forced to watch. More quietly, the Taliban carried out mass murder of members of non-Pashtun ethnic groups, often selling women into slavery. They cultivated poppies for the heroin trade and destroyed World Heritage cultural artefacts, most notably the giant Bamyan Buddha statues from the sixth century. Their oppression of women was fanatical, and they ruled conquered populations by terror. The Taliban sheltered Osama bin Laden, founder of the militant Islamic organisation al-Qaeda. In return, al-Qaeda provided the Taliban with fighters. Soon after the terror attacks of 11 September 2001 (known as 9/11), the US invaded Afghanistan, ostensibly clearing the country of the Taliban by December. This proved to be an illusion: many years later, the US is still fighting the Taliban in Afghanistan.

The Pakistani military and ISI were instrumental in supporting the Taliban throughout their fight for control in Afghanistan and – though it is denied – well after Pakistan ostensibly allied itself with the US against al-Qaeda and the Taliban in 2001. In 2007, a Pakistani Taliban, called the TTP (Tehrik-i-Taliban-Pakistan, or 'Taliban Movement of Pakistan') formed. Though technically separate from the Afghani Taliban, the TTP is dedicated to bringing the same form of sharia law to Pakistan. This is discussed in great detail in *I Am Malala*. Maulana Fazlullah became the leader of the TTP in late 2013. He was killed by a US air strike in Afghanistan in June 2018.

GENRE, STRUCTURE & LANGUAGE

Genre

I Am Malala is a memoir. Unlike autobiographies (which often cover a whole lifetime), memoirs tend to focus on related episodes or single themes in a life. Although *I Am Malala* covers all her existence to the time of writing, Malala Yousafzai – now only in her early twenties – is daily adding experiences. As time passes, the book will seem more like a prologue than a summation. Memoirs can call on any number of literary conventions, but most often they read like novels in the sense that they use multiple developed characters, intricate plots, well-described settings and plenty of dialogue. Always popular, the memoir has become one of the dominant literary forms. Those written by famous people have a built-in audience most novelists can only dream of. In the period after her shooting in 2012, Malala was one of the best-known people on the planet. There would have been fierce competition to publish the story of the brave campaigner for girls' rights shot by one of the most hated groups in the world.

Audiences and critics generally expect memoirs and biographies to be scrupulous about facts, and hold their authors to very high standards in relation to objectivity. Some of the biggest literary controversies in the recent past have started as accusations against memoirists for fabricating elements of their stories. Memoirists cannot hide behind the same defences that novelists can, in terms of separating narrators' opinions from their own, or claiming that their writing is fiction rather than fact.

As readers we should ask who the intended audience for any text is, and then evaluate it in that context. This is particularly true for memoirs written by public figures, who might be attempting to satisfy a range of different interests. As you read this work, consider who the possible audiences are, what the authors are hoping to achieve for each of them, and how this might influence the story being told and the way it is told.

Who is Malala?

There are many possible intended audiences for *I Am Malala*: politicians and policy makers; human rights activists; children interested in history, politics or religion; students who are assigned this text whether they're interested or not; Westerners baffled, intrigued or repulsed by the ways of strict Islamic communities; Muslims who approve of Malala's stance against the Taliban; Muslims who disapprove of it; readers simply interested in 'The Girl Who Stood Up for Education and Was Shot by the Taliban'.

Some of the writing in this book aims to reconcile, or at least address, the biggest gap between these multiple audiences – for example between Westerners who know about Malala's shooting but little about her life, and readers back in Pakistan (or in other Islamic countries) who had possibly formed an opinion about her even before she was shot. *I Am Malala* seems most focused on appealing to audiences from her two homes: the Swat Valley of Pakistan, and Birmingham, the UK's second-largest city.

The question first asked by the gunman who nearly killed her ('Who is Malala?') is used as the jumping-off point for Malala's story. But the answer to the question is not simple. The authors (generally referred to in this guide in the singular, as Malala, since the narrative is in Malala's voice, although it is important to remember that Christina Lamb, a veteran journalist, would have done much of the writing) take great pains to write both for Western and non-Western readers. As you read the memoir, ask yourself questions such as: when is Malala trying to appeal to the Pashtuns of Swat? When is she, instead, writing in accordance with the values of Birmingham? How do these intentions influence the narrative decisions and language choices in the text?

Structure

The narrative of *I Am Malala* follows the order of events in its subject's life, with one minor but significant deviation. The prologue offers a sense of immediacy, with the initial entry point into the story being 9 October 2012, the day that Malala was shot by Ataullah Khan as she rode home from school on a small bus. The shooting is the one thing that most readers already know about Malala, so addressing it at the very beginning is likely to draw readers in. Once the prologue is finished, the narrative reverts to a basic chronological order (including the early lives of her parents), revisiting the day of the shooting about three-quarters of the way through and proceeding to the time of the writing.

Running parallel to the personal and public events of Malala's life is a history of Pakistan as a nation and of Swat. The writing about the latter is quite introspective; Malala has a deep and genuine love for her beautiful, abused homeland. The Pakistani history, on the other hand, provides important context to the events of her life, even while some of the details appear far removed from the Yousafzais' daily realities.

Language

The language of *I Am Malala* is journalistic in style. It uses very few metaphors, and limited poetic devices within the prose. It is literal and concrete, intended to convey information rather than generate literary artistry. The authors also tend to let facts speak for themselves, generally avoiding the use of emotive language to arouse the reader's sympathy (although there are occasional exceptions, such as when Malala relates her feelings about her valley). One brief deviation from the pragmatic language occurs in Chapter 20, when Malala describes the moments leading up to her shooting. It is as if time slows down. The narrative takes in everyday features of her home town (a red tricycle, a man chopping off chicken's heads, p.202) in a level of detail reminiscent of a novel. This contrasts with the language choices elsewhere in the text.

There are many Pashtun words in *I Am Malala*, which are mostly defined at first use and presented in italic font. Some of these describe concepts unique to Pashtun or Pakistani culture, while others are the Pashtun equivalents of English ideas. A glossary is provided for the most-used terms (pp.267–9). (Note that there are also some definitions provided in this guide, in the 'Vocabulary for writing on *I Am Malala*' section.) One of the aims of this book is to humanise a part of the world that many readers would know little about: any knowledge they do have about the area is likely to have originated in Western stereotypes of Islamic fundamentalism. By using the Pashtun words (including those for ideas or concepts readers might already be familiar with in English), Malala is both bringing her culture to the forefront and asserting her sense of her own identity: she is a Pashtun woman first and a world figure second.

Style

Like most contemporary memoirs, the style of *I Am Malala* differs little from that of a realist novel. Characters' dialogue and behaviour is reported as though it is exactly what took place, even when the events occurred many years before the writing of the text. This is a stylistic approach most memoirs follow, and requires a certain suspension of disbelief on the reader's part: of course, the narrative is reconstructed by the author even while it is a telling of 'real' events. Remember also that there are two authors at work here, Malala Yousafzai and Christina Lamb. There are times when we hear the first's voice quite distinctly – for example in Malala's impassioned words about education, or her gossipy asides about friends. At other times, we are likely to attribute the content to the professional journalist's voice – such as in the more complex and detailed sections on Pakistani history. Christina Lamb undoubtedly conducted many interviews, not just with Malala but with other figures from her life. The influence of this is clearly evident in the work, and it is possible to guess who Lamb's main sources might have been. Sometimes apparently minor characters are given more space in the memoir, while there are important characters whose voice we never hear. One example is Malala's best friend Moniba, who remains completely silent – except for the things Malala says *about* her. Toor Pekai is another character from whom we rarely hear directly in the novel. Toor Pekai was there throughout Malala's life, making all the family's domestic decisions – but compared to the narrative input of Malala's father, who was often physically absent from the home, Toor Pekai's voice is virtually nonexistent. These silences may be a result of authorial decisions, or they may be the more pragmatic result of the constraints placed on women in Pashtun society. Was Moniba kept from speaking to Christina Lamb by her brothers – or even by her own interpretations of Muslim propriety? Similarly, a devout believer in purdah, Malala's mother may have been unwilling to talk very much.

Ziauddin, however, is everywhere. Malala clearly idolises her father, and they have a very close personal relationship as well as a team approach to working towards their shared beliefs and goals. With Toor Pekai at home in purdah, Ziauddin was the only possible source of outside information for his daughter, so it makes sense that his role in Malala's life is an influential one. Thus he is a significant part of Malala's story, and not just of the narrative of the text but of the style in which it is conveyed.

CHAPTER-BY-CHAPTER ANALYSIS

Preface (pp. xvii–xxiii)

Summary: *Writing one year after the publication of* I Am Malala, *the authors describe Malala's life as a seventeen-year-old in Birmingham, England, and her activism since leaving Pakistan.*

Malala and her family resettle in Birmingham following the attempt on her life in Pakistan. The changes in the lives of the Yousafzais are presented as largely positive – Ziauddin takes care of the family by shopping and cooking for them 'like a woman, a true feminist' (p.xvii) while Malala's mother has her first experience of formal education, learning English at a language centre. Malala, too, is busy with her studies, which she finds unexpectedly challenging compared to her schooling in Pakistan. While she is happy to embrace this challenge, it demonstrates that adjusting to her new life in Birmingham is not always easy for her. She misses her Pakistani friends and her beloved Swat, and still faces some physical challenges following her recovery from injury.

Malala's continuing activism helps to distract her from her homesickness. She describes her work with the Malala Fund, visits to Kenya, Nigeria and the Syrian border, and meeting the then US President, Barack Obama. This activity indicates her continuing commitment to fighting for education for children around the world.

Q *I Am Malala* begins and ends with Malala's life in Birmingham. How does this circular structure contribute to your understanding of Malala's statement, 'My life has changed, but I have not'?

Prologue: The Day My World Changed (pp.1–6)

Summary: *The memoir's central event, the attempt on Malala's life as she returns home from school, occurs.*

The gunman's question to the group of students on the bus – 'Who is Malala? (p.6) – is cleverly repurposed by the authors at the end of this chapter. The Taliban thought they knew exactly who Malala was: a defiant girl who refused to conform to their interpretations of Islam; an activist who would not be silent. To them, Malala was nothing more than the girl who deserved death.

By turning that same question, 'who is Malala?', into the starting point for her memoir, Malala foreshadows traits that will become apparent in the book: that she refuses to have her identity erased by threats and that she will not lock herself away and out of sight as the Taliban demand (note that Malala is the only girl on the bus with her 'face not covered', p.6). Prejudice, such as this Taliban gunman displays, reduces the identity of others to stereotypes. Telling her story in detail allows Malala to defy those whose reason for asking, 'Who is Malala?' is purely to make sure they kill the right person.

Q Anticipating what her reaction would be if anyone tried to kill her, Malala thinks, 'maybe I'd take off my shoes and hit him, but then I'd think if I did that there would be no difference between me and a terrorist' (p.4). Do you think this is true? Why or why not?

PART ONE: Before the Taliban

Chapter 1: A Daughter Is Born (pp.9–20)

Summary: *Malala tells us about the members of her immediate family; her homeland, the Swat Valley of Pakistan; her people, the Pashtuns; and some of their traditions.*

Ziauddin Yousafzai differs from typical Pashtun men by celebrating the birth of his daughter (most men only celebrate the birth of a son); usually 'daughters are hidden away behind a curtain, their role in life simply to prepare food and give birth to children' (p.9). Pashtun culture is male-dominated. Family and personal honour are paramount, and offences are avenged with violence.

There will be a tension throughout this memoir between Malala's activism for the rights of girls and her love for a culture that oppresses them. It is notable that Ziauddin – who will prove as much a champion of girls' rights to education as his daughter – asks people to celebrate his daughter's birth not because girls are as important as boys but because, he asserts, 'there is something different about this child' (p.9). He names her Malala, after 'the greatest heroine of Afghanistan' (p.9), the Pashtuns' 'Joan of Arc' (p.10). Right from her birth there is a kind of myth-making about Malala.

Key point

Perhaps as a result of this tension between activism and faith, the memoir swings between two competing urges: to portray Malala as a typical Pashtun girl, or to portray her as someone 'different', a child apart, chosen by destiny to become a second 'Joan of Arc'.

Malala describes the Swat Valley, which is sometimes known as the 'Switzerland of the East' as 'the most beautiful place in all the world' (p.11). Isolated by the mountains surrounding it, the valley has a history of self-rule. It is part of Pakistan, but also a world unto itself – echoing the multiple identities the Pashtuns themselves experience. As Malala writes, 'like all Swatis I thought of myself first as Swati and then Pashtun, before Pakistani' (p.20).

Q Both Malala and her father are ashamed of their dark skin (p.16). What does this tell you about Malala's family and culture?

Chapter 2: My Father the Falcon (pp.21–31)

Summary: *Ziauddin's early life is discussed, in parallel with the early years of Pakistan.*

Malala's father grew up in extreme poverty. He was tormented for his stutter by his domineering father – Malala's *baba* (grandfather) – a teacher and *imam* (leader of prayers at a mosque) famous for his lectures and sermons. The chapter ends with young Ziauddin turning 'his weakness into strength' and earning his father's respect by winning a public-speaking competition (p.31), something Malala will do herself in Chapter 5. Before devoting himself to education, though, Ziauddin flirted with extremist positions under the tutelage of a *talib* (religious student). Malala conjectures that Ziauddin's lack of prospects made him susceptible to 'brainwashing' (p.27), inclining him to believe in martyrdom and jihad (holy war).

Though Pakistan came into being on a wave of optimism, it soon descended into violence and autocracy. The years under the military dictatorship of General Zia (beginning when Ziauddin was eight) saw the country retreat to a fundamentalist and intolerant Islam. This included repressive treatment of women – for example, rape laws that required the testimony of four men for a conviction (p.24).

Q Considering his later resistance to the Taliban, how does the revelation that Ziauddin also had a 'fundamentalist' phase as a young man influence your understanding of his character?

Chapter 3: Growing Up in a School (pp.32–46)

Summary: *We learn of the many difficulties Ziauddin faced as he tried to realise his 'dream' (p.32) of opening his first school.*

The travails detailed here – from money problems, to family problems, to corrupt school inspectors, to multiple floods inundating his building – would have defeated a less optimistic or determined man than Malala's father. At the beginning of the chapter we learn of the education of

Malala's mother, Toor Pekai. Unlike most Pashtun girls, she was at least encouraged to go to school by her father, but she did less than one term, when she was six. 'There seemed no point in going to school just to end up cooking, cleaning and bringing up children, so one day she sold her books' (p.32). This provides a contrast with Malala's beliefs about education. At the end of the chapter, Malala recalls the turmoil surrounding the events of September 2001: 'we did not realise then that 9/11 would change our world too' (p.46). Her insular perspective on her homeland is intruded upon by the wider world.

Q What do the different educational journeys of Malala's two parents say about the differences between girls and boys in Pashtun society?

Chapter 4: The Village (pp.47–55)

Summary: *Malala describes the time spent at her father's small village in the mountains for the Eid festivals.*

There is some evocative writing in this chapter on the beauty of great mountains, contrasting with some of the concrete language used to describe the historical and political context. The villages themselves, 'forgotten' places (p.51), are tiny and backward. There are no hospitals, and children sometimes freeze to death in wattle and daub houses (p.51). With little work available, many of the men have had to leave in order to make money in the dangerous coal mines in the south of the country, or to work in construction in the far-off states of the Persian Gulf. As a young child, Malala loves the change of scenery and the chance to spend festive times with extended family. The girls play games relating to wedding customs, reminding us that marriage and motherhood are the only prospects many Pashtun girls have (pp.52–3).

As she gets older, Malala starts to find the villages boring. Her choice not to veil herself also attracts unwanted judgement. She is accused of 'not properly following *Pashtunwali*' (p.54). Malala gives examples of the crimes that this code abets: selling girls as young as ten to much older men; the murder of girls by their family for flirting; the giving of girls in marriage in order to settle family disputes. Malala's father asserts that things like this will not be allowed to happen to her: 'I will protect your freedom, Malala. Carry on with your dreams' (p.55).

Q When Malala complains to her father of the oppression of women in their culture, he responds that life is 'harder for women in Afghanistan' (p.55). In what ways does the text support this assertion?

Chapter 5: Why I Don't Wear Earrings and Pashtuns Don't Say Thank You (pp.56–64)

Summary: *Malala recalls a brief period when she stole jewellery from her friend Safina; this leads to more discussion of* Pashtunwali.

This incident reveals aspects of Malala's character. To begin with, she is not a person to do things in half measures. Convinced that Safina stole one of her favourite toys, Malala seems determined to steal *all* of Safina's possessions, one at a time. It becomes a 'compulsion' (p.57). Caught, she is shamed by her mother, who rejects Malala's justifications ('Safina started it'): 'Safina is younger than you … You should have set an example' (p.57). Malala repents what she has done, and – again, showing her tendency towards all-or-nothing behaviour – decides that she will *never* wear jewellery again. She also concludes that 'everyone makes a mistake at least once in their life. The important thing is what you learn from it' (p.59).

However, learning from mistakes is not how the *Pashtunwali* operates. Never forgetting, never forgiving (p.59), the code demands revenge for perceived wrongs, even mistakes. The Pashtuns are a feuding people, ensnared by eternal grudges pitting entire families against others – and even, in the horrific example of Sher Zaman (p.60), revenge against one's own cousins.

Key point

Malala initially tries to justify her theft as an act of vengeance, as the *Pashtunwali* code would seem to demand. Repenting of her deed, she is, in a larger sense, signalling her rejection of the code. One of the great men Ziauddin cites when he tries to console Malala is Gandhi ('Freedom is not worth having if it does not include the freedom to make mistakes', pp.58–9). Gandhi was the great exemplar of nonviolent resistance, the method that Malala herself favours as an activist.

Q Do you think Malala's vow *never* to wear jewellery again is too extreme? Why or why not?

Chapter 6: Children of the Rubbish Mountain (pp.65–73)

Summary: *Malala takes up the cause of educating the destitute children of the rubbish tip.*

A lesson of this chapter is that advocacy can be scary at first, but then can take over your life. Malala is frightened by the ragged girl she sees picking through rubbish at the dump; but soon she becomes obsessed with helping her and the others. She pleads with her father to allow these lost children to come to his school for free. Ziauddin already allocates free places at his school to deprived children – a kindness that costs him twice when rich parents start pulling their children out, rather than suffer the 'shame' of contact with the children of their servants (p.67). Ziauddin decides to write and print a pamphlet on the issue instead (p.68).

While this is not necessarily a useless endeavour, it stands in contrast to the kind of practical actions Malala's mother takes in similar situations. The chapter refers to some of the many poor children Toor Pekai takes into the family home to live or to receive necessary meals ('wherever we lived my mother filled our house with people', p.66). In contrast to the varying kinds of altruism displayed by her parents, Malala examines more of the corruption current in Swat and in Pakistan. The Pakistani dictator Pervez Musharraf pockets much of the billions of dollars the US gives to the nation to fight the Taliban – 'while still helping the jihadis' (p. 71). Wealthy insiders in Swat take money from the government to set up schools that never eventuate (p.68).

The chapter begins and ends with prayers Malala sends to God. In the first, she desires a magic pencil from a popular cartoon so that she can 'make everyone happy' (p.65). In the second, she asks God: 'make me perfect because I want to make this world perfect' (p.72).

Q How are Malala's prayers in keeping with what we've learned about her so far?

Chapter 7: The *Mufti* Who Tried to Close Our School (pp.74–83)

Summary: *Ziauddin experiences fundamentalist interference with his school.*

Malala's father gets the better of a *mufti* (Islamic legal scholar) who insists that the girls' school he is running is *haram* (forbidden by Islam). It is a preview of the much more terrifying pressure he will come under when the Taliban move into the Swat Valley. Elections in 2002, at a time when the US was at war against the Taliban in Afghanistan, bring a fundamentalist government to Swat: 'It was as though they wanted to remove all traces of womankind from public life' (p.80).

Q Mullah Ghulamullah asserts that girls should not be allowed to go to school because they are too 'sacred' to be allowed out in public. What does this suggest about the Taliban's view of women?

Chapter 8: The Autumn of the Earthquake (pp.84–8)

Summary: *An earthquake hits the Swat Valley and Pakistan.*

In later chapters, Malala relates how fundamentalist forces, including the new Swati Taliban, use this catastrophe – which killed more than 70 000 people – to frighten Muslims into embracing fundamentalist views (for example on p.92). Welfare wings of militant organisations like the Lashkar-e-Taiba send volunteers to aid victims and set up a field hospital, succeeding where the Pakistani government fails (p.87). Orphaned children, whom the government promises to take care of, are instead enrolled in *madrasas* where they are indoctrinated in fundamentalist dogma (p.88).

Q Why do you think militant organisations would take part in disaster relief?

PART TWO: The Valley of Death

Chapter 9: Radio Mullah (pp.91–101)

Summary: *The Taliban come to Swat.*

At first, many of the people of Mingora find the Taliban appealing; they listen to the radio program of the leader, Maulana Fazlullah, and follow his advice on leading a pious life. The broadcasts gradually become harsh and judgemental of people or systems most listeners dislike. ('They liked his talk of bringing back Islamic law as everyone was frustrated with the Pakistani justice system', p.93). Fazlullah attacks 'the injustice of the feudal system of the khans' (hereditary lords) and is seen 'as a kind of Robin Hood' who will 'give the khans' land to the poor' (p.94). As Ziauddin's friend Hidayatullah explains: 'they want to win the hearts and minds of the people', but 'when they get power, they behave like the criminals they once hunted down' (p.94).

Soon Fazlullah is adjudicating disputes and sending out violent squads to ensure citizens are following his extreme edicts regarding behaviour. At Eid, the killing starts: 'khans and political activists from secular and nationalist parties' are murdered (p.99). The local authorities do nothing to stop them. Ziauddin returns from the holidays to find a threatening letter attached to his school's gate. He responds with a courageous letter in the local newspaper: 'you can take my life but please don't kill my schoolchildren' (p.101).

Q Ziauddin laments how Fazlullah spreads ignorance (p.94). How do others view Fazlullah, and why do you think this is?

Chapter 10: Toffees, Tennis Balls and the Buddhas of Swat (pp.102–11)

Summary: *The Taliban cracks down in Swat, and Pakistan begins to come apart.*

The Taliban destroy Swat's beloved statues of Buddha. They destroy televisions and even children's games. They kill policemen, compelling others to flee in fear. 'All this happened and nobody did a thing. It was as though everyone was in a trance' (p.103). The Taliban have also moved into Islamabad, Pakistan's capital. Benazir Bhutto, the female former prime minister and one of Malala's idols, is assassinated soon after returning to Pakistan from exile. Malala writes, 'it was because of Benazir that girls like me could think of speaking out and becoming politicians' (p.107). But girls are also speaking out in the cause of intolerance. Girls from the Red Mosque *madrasa*, dressed in burqas (full body veils) and under the sway of the Taliban, start terrorising citizens in Islamabad. The army moves into Swat and seems to drive the Taliban out, but no-one believes they are gone for good.

Q Is it consistent with the Taliban's philosophy that they would encourage girls to become martyrs?

Chapter 11: The Clever Class (pp.112–22)

Summary: *During a stalemate between the army and the Taliban, Malala is able to continue her studies; she begins doing interviews for television and radio.*

The army remains in Swat, yet Fazlullah continues his radio broadcasts. The Taliban start blowing up schools and encouraging suicide bombers to terrorise the population. One kills fifty-five people, including several from the family of Malala's friend Moniba (p.114). It is thought that Swat is being 'sacrificed' to the Taliban to keep them out of the rest of Pakistan (p.116). Ziauddin speaks out against the Taliban at every opportunity; Malala decides to make a stand, too. Her words regarding her decision to give national television interviews (p.117) are revealing: they illustrate some of the beliefs behind her activism.

Key point

Here, as elsewhere, Malala seems cautious about her motivations. We need to remember that this book is written not just for Western readers, but many who would condemn her presumption in speaking out, simply because of her gender and youth. Before admitting to her ambition and remarkable self-belief (*'If one man, Fazlullah, can destroy everything, why can't one girl change it?'*, p.117), Malala makes sure she asserts that she was speaking out only with her father's permission, and out of a 'duty' to 'God' (p.117).

Q How does Malala's declaration about her education (p.122) differ from her mother's decision to stop attending school decades earlier (p.32)?

Chapter 12: The Bloody Square (pp.123–8)

Summary: *The Taliban kill with impunity and dump the bodies in Mingora's Green Chowk.*

Malala uses the case of Shabana, murdered by the Taliban for being a dancer, as a way to analyse the grip that Fazlullah's group maintains over the people of Swat: 'terror had made people cruel. The Taliban bulldozed both our Pashtun values and the values of Islam' (p.128). Earlier in the chapter she criticises some of those Pashtun values:

> We Pashtuns love shoes but don't love the cobbler … Manual workers made a great contribution to our society but received no recognition, and this is the reason so many of them joined the Taliban – to finally achieve status and power. (p.124)

Men are murdered for wearing their pants too long; policemen are beheaded for staying in their jobs. The state of terror becomes so great that the people of Mingora start seeing conspiracies everywhere. Most assume that, rather than confronting the Taliban, the army is secretly supporting them, so many send the young men in their family to join the Taliban: 'it seemed that people had decided the Taliban were here to stay and they had better get along with them' (p.125).

Q What do you think of the reasoning in this chapter? Does the text suggest that 'status and power' are the main reasons young men join the Taliban, or that the people just want to 'get along'? (Support your answer with evidence from the chapter.)

Chapter 13: The Diary of Gul Makai (pp.129–37)

Summary: *Malala is prompted to start keeping a blog of her life under the Taliban, modelled on the famous diary of Anne Frank.*

The desire to expose the Taliban is laudable, but there are challenges inherent in the journalist Abdul Hai Kakar's attempt to manufacture a Pashtun Anne Frank. Anne Frank's diary was hidden, while Malala's blog is dictated for immediate international distribution. The situations of the two families also differed significantly. The Yousafzais could have conformed to the Taliban's demands – unpalatable as that might have been – and continued living unmolested; they were also free to leave the Swat Valley. Conversely, Jews like the Franks under German occupation could not simply conform to the occupiers' expectations, and to escape as refugees became increasingly difficult for Jews.

While Malala may not have been aware of the differences between Anne Frank's situation and her own, she nonetheless found the diary a challenge. She admits that 'I wanted to tell people it was me … I almost gave the game away … when I said … my real name means "grief-stricken"' (p.131). Malala's dedication to her task was characteristic of her determination to fight oppression. Her courage and composure are remarkable, particularly for a girl of her age.

Q This chapter is about Malala's first exposure to international attention, through blogs, videos and interviews. What role do you think ambition plays in her fame?

Chapter 14: A Funny Kind of Peace (pp.138–46)

Summary: *The Taliban and the provincial government sign a truce.*

Malala has started attending school secretly, amid Taliban threats, when she finds out that a truce has been reached. There is great celebration, but the Yousafzais are cautious. Their concerns are shown to be justified when the Taliban continue exactly as before, terrorising the inhabitants of Swat and violently enforcing extreme religious laws. 'The Taliban believed the Pakistani government had given in and they could do what they liked' (p.145).

The Taliban occupation of a province near Swat becomes too much for the government. The military launches an operation, first telling everyone to leave the Swat Valley.

Q Ziauddin had always refused to flee in dangerous times. Do you think his statement that they should stay in defiance of the army's announcement is courageous or foolish? Why?

Chapter 15: Leaving the Valley (pp.147–54)

Summary: *The family flees the Swat Valley.*

In the end it is Malala's mother who forces their departure, giving Ziauddin an ultimatum: 'You don't have to come, but I am going and I will take the children to Shangla' (p.148). It is the 'biggest exodus in Pashtun history' (p.149) and, in accordance with *Pashtunwali*, hundreds of thousands of refugees are taken in by the inhabitants of Mardan. After the first night, Ziauddin decides to go to Peshawar to spread the word about the conditions the refugees are facing.

The rest of the journey proves arduous and fraught with danger – Toor Pekai has to beat off a man with her shoe (p.151) – but they make it to Shangla, where Malala attends school with her cousin Sumbul. In the end, Ziauddin does not come to Shangla at all, staying in Peshawar, where the family journeys to meet him.

Q The twenty-four chapters of *I Am Malala* are divided into five parts. Why do you think the authors chose to organise the book in this way? How do the section divisions enhance your understanding of Malala's story?

PART THREE: Three Girls, Three Bullets

Chapter 16: The Valley of Sorrows (pp.157–70)

Summary: *The family returns to the Swat Valley; flooding disrupts life once again.*

Malala is overjoyed to return to school soon after the family returns to Mingora. The city has been disfigured by the fighting, but the Yousafzais' house is unharmed. Ziauddin finds that his school had been occupied by soldiers of the army, who left notes blaming the people of Swat for the ascent of the Taliban and for forcing sacrifice by the army to remove them. He protests the unfairness of these accusations: 'we people of Swat were first seduced by the Taliban, then killed by them and now blamed for them' (p.159).

Malala and some friends take part in workshops in Islamabad based on their experience with the Taliban. In the capital, she meets 'women who were lawyers and doctors and also activists, which showed us that women could do important jobs yet still keep their culture and traditions' (p.162).

Back in Swat, life seems to be returning to normal when the valley, and all of Pakistan, is hit with unprecedented floods. Once again the fundamentalist organisations are more involved than the government in relief efforts. Soon the Taliban are blowing up schools again and carrying out assassinations.

Q Does the text suggest that the people of Swat bear any responsibility for the Taliban takeover? Why or why not?

Chapter 17: Praying to Be Tall (pp.171–82)

Summary: *Malala wins Pakistan's first National Peace Prize.*

Two sensational murders – of Punjabi governor Salman Taseer by his own bodyguard and of Osama bin Laden by American special forces – roil Pakistan. Malala is alarmed by the widespread approval in Pakistan of the first killing (Taseer had suggested liberalising blasphemy laws). The nation itself is up in arms about the US violating its sovereignty in the second. Ziauddin, who begins advocating for women whose husbands have disappeared in the recent military incursions against the Taliban (p.172), is furious that the ISI had evidently been sheltering bin Laden, the world's most wanted terrorist, for years.

Pakistan's government begins to seriously recognise Malala. Not only does she win the nation's inaugural peace prize, but it is decided that the prize should be named after her. It comes with a large cash reward, as do a number of other such prizes she wins, making the family ostensibly wealthy. Malala calls these awards 'little jewels without much meaning' (p.181) and uses the bulk of the money to begin an education foundation dedicated to helping girls in poverty.

Q Are Malala's prizes really 'jewels without much meaning'? What meaning do they have besides monetary value?

Chapter 18: The Woman and the Sea (pp.183–9)

Summary: *Malala receives a death threat.*

In Karachi, Pakistan's largest city, Malala reflects on some problems facing her country. Her aunt, who has lived on the coast for three decades, has never seen the sea – because her husband would not take her: 'we were a country where almost all the women depend entirely on men' (p.183). The nation's founder, Mohammad Ali Jinnah, had envisioned an 'important role' for women (p.186), but died a year after Pakistan's independence. Jinnah 'wanted everyone to be free whatever their beliefs' (p.187), but the country has become divided by ethnicity and sectarian animosities.

Malala finds out that the Taliban, who have officially been driven out of Swat, have issued a death threat against her (p.188). She insists that she is not afraid to die, but remarks to her father, 'when there was Talibanisation we were safe; now there are no Taliban and we are unsafe' (p.189). Her father responds, 'now the Talibanisation is especially for us, for those ... who continue to speak out' (p.189).

Q The title of this chapter refers to more than just Malala's Aunt Najma. What does it have to do with Malala herself, and Pakistan's women in general?

Chapter 19: A Private Talibanisation (pp.190–7)

Summary: *Threats against Ziauddin become more severe.*

The family discovers what it means to be targeted specifically, as opposed to being members of a group under threat. Ziauddin's school is subject to a propaganda campaign suggesting it encourages immoral behaviour, and the family is repeatedly questioned by people who seem to be intelligence agents. Ziauddin's life comes under direct threat when his friend and colleague, Zahid Khan, is shot.

Key point

Ziauddin speaks out not only against the Taliban, but also against the military. Like Zahid Khan (p.196), he is convinced that the Taliban could not have gained a foothold in the Swat Valley without the approval of the ISI and the army itself. As another friend says of the Taliban, they are 'a mentality, and this mentality is everywhere in Pakistan' (p.194).

Q How does Malala's response to the love letter she receives from neighbourhood boy Haroon fit with what you have learned about her character so far?

Chapter 20: Who is Malala? (pp.198–203)

Summary: *The narrative returns to 9 October 2012, the day of the shooting.*

More detail is given of the days leading up to the assassination attempt. Some of the language and stylistic choices in this chapter are less concrete and more figurative than the writing elsewhere, such as the use of symbolism and foreshadowing. Malala's van passes a 'wanted' poster of Fazlullah just before it is stopped by his two hitmen; Malala's fingers drum to the rhythm of a man chopping the heads off chickens. 'Funny, when I was little we always said Swatis were so peace-loving it was hard to find a man to slaughter a chicken', she reflects (p.202). Things have changed: now some Swati men are willing to slaughter fifteen-year-old girls.

Q Malala asserts that she and her family 'believe in God more than they [the Taliban] do' (p.199). Why do you think this point is so important to her?

PART FOUR: Between Life and Death

Chapter 21: 'God, I entrust her to you' (pp.207–19)

Summary: *The chaotic few hours after the shooting.*

As in Chapter 15 – when he leaves his refugee family to find their way to Shangla without him – Ziauddin's behaviour here reveals his dedication to his beliefs even when this compromises his commitment to his family. Informed that his school's bus has been fired upon, Malala's father decides to carry on giving the speech he was set to make to a conference of principals. Only then does he go to the hospital.

Other key characters' responses similarly illustrate aspects of their personality. Toor Pekai's first action is to rush back to her home and start praying. Madam Maryam, Malala's headmistress, gets to the hospital on the back of her husband's motorbike – even a respected teacher would not be permitted to go there unaccompanied. Malala is flown to Peshawar for proper treatment. Ziauddin and Madam Maryam (acting in the role of 'mother') accompany her in the helicopter. At the Combined Military Hospital, Malala is operated on by military neurosurgeon Colonel Junaid. His 'brave' (p.214) decision to remove some of Malala's skull as her brain was swelling saves her life.

The Taliban take responsibility for the shooting, saying that Malala was targeted not because of her efforts for girls' rights, but because she was promoting 'secularism' and 'Western culture' (p.216). General Kayani, the head of the military, takes it upon himself to oversee Malala's care – at first Ziauddin is worried, as he does not trust the military, but the General seems to have Malala's best interests in mind. Her condition deteriorates. Two doctors visiting Pakistan from Birmingham examine her. They approve of the operation done on Malala, but not of the postoperative care.

Chapter 22: Journey into the Unknown (pp.220–8)

Summary: *The world follows the case as Malala is flown to England for treatment.*

The possibility that Malala might die under military care brings increased international pressure to send her to a Western country. General Kayani is adamant that she will not be treated or transported by Americans (p.225), with whom relations are strained. The nation seems as concerned about 'losing face' as about Malala's life. Eventually a solution is found: Malala will be flown to England by the ruling family of the United Arab Emirates.

Ziauddin is told that he must accompany Malala, but he refuses, saying that his wife and two sons would be without their protector if he did. He gives his permission for Dr Fiona, one of the doctors from Birmingham, to become her temporary guardian.

Q What role do you think fame played in Malala's treatment and her ultimate survival?

PART FIVE: A Second Life

Chapter 23: 'The Girl Shot in the Head, Birmingham' (pp.231–44)

Summary: *Malala is without her parents for ten days in hospital in Birmingham.*

Malala is very confused and unable to speak in the first few days after waking up in the English hospital. Her most persistent thoughts are to do with her absent father – no doubt influenced not just by her closeness to him but also the fact that, in Pakistan, she could not be out of the home like this without her father or another male relative being present – and with money: Malala becomes almost obsessed with how her hospital stay will be paid for. She is comforted by an Urdu-speaking female chaplain, but feels very out of place, despite the good intentions of the hospital staff.

After being informed of what happened, Malala says that she didn't feel any desire for revenge against her assailants: 'my only regret was that I hadn't had a chance to speak to them before they shot me' (p.237).

Q Do you think this regret speaks more to Malala's powers of forgiveness, or to her belief in her powers of persuasion?

Q What does Malala's reaction to the film *Bend it like Beckham* tell you about her?

Chapter 24: 'They have snatched her smile' (pp.245–55)

Summary: *Malala's parents finally arrive.*

Though her parents try to disguise their reaction upon seeing her – her hair has been shaved, and her face is partially paralysed – Malala is upset that they are so shocked. 'I reassured my mother that it did not matter to me if my face was not symmetrical … when you see death, things change' (p.246).

Ziauddin asks his wife if it is his fault that Malala was nearly killed. Toor Pekai, who has always been worried about Malala's exposure to danger, is remarkably forgiving: 'You didn't send Malala out thieving or killing or to commit crimes. It was a noble cause' (p.247).

An operation to fix Malala's facial nerve is successful. After a few months, her smile returns. She reflects on the journey of her life so far, and reasserts to the reader her devotion to God, and her commitment to helping others:

> It feels like this life is a second life. People prayed to God to spare me, and I was spared for a reason – to use my life for helping people. (p.255)

Q To what extent do you think Malala's father is to blame for her injuries and her exposure to danger?

Epilogue: One Child, One Teacher, One Book, One Pen … (pp.256–65)

Summary: *Nearly a year after the shooting, Malala reflects on her life in Birmingham.*

This chapter intends to disabuse readers of the idea that Malala must be happy in her new modern, peaceful and (relatively) tolerant country. In fact, the family is having a hard time adjusting. Used to a house full of the relatives and poor families she's taken in, Toor Pekai is lonely. Ziauddin has to deal with the widely held opinion that he pushed Malala into her activism 'like a tennis dad trying to create a champion' (p.258). He also misses his political projects and the school he built up over decades. Malala misses her classmates and is having difficulty adjusting to her new school.

As Pakistan slips deeper into chaos and violence, many of her countrymen slander her, saying that Malala got what she was seeking all along, 'a life of luxury abroad' (p.262). Some deny that she was shot. It all makes Malala more determined that others should not dictate how she lives; she will use her 'second life' fully by championing the rights of children.

CHARACTERS & RELATIONSHIPS

Malala Yousafzai

Key quotes

'I will protect your freedom, Malala. Carry on with your dreams.' (Ziauddin, p.55)

'God, give me strength and courage and make me perfect because I want to make this world perfect …' (p.72)

'I was speaking up for my rights as a Muslim woman to be able to go to school.' (p.238)

Real people can be more complicated than fictional characters. Does *I Am Malala* satisfy the question used as its point of departure, 'Who is Malala'? Yes and no. While the book contains vast amounts of information, some areas are under-explored or obscured. There are some things we never learn about Malala, even while her character is painstakingly constructed through small details and events.

Malala's has been a life of sacrifice, as are those of many people as devoted as she is to worthy causes. However, her actions alone do not wholly account for the impact Malala has had on world opinion. To some extent, it is also her individual personality that has allowed her to achieve what she has achieved. For example, there is no question that Malala possesses incredible courage, integrity and intelligence. Her devotion to education rights, to her parents and to God are also evident. Though now a 'world figure', her love for the Swat Valley is palpable and her exile is an obvious source of pain. All these elements have contributed to her public life as an activist.

Western readers looking for a feminist icon might be puzzled by Malala's unquestioning devotion to her father, her overly cautious criticisms of a *Pashtunwali* code that seems so vicious to women, and her total commitment to a religion whose teachings can be so easily distorted to justify crimes in the Swat Valley and elsewhere. These qualities might be criticised as creating a tension within her identity. Yet Malala did not set out to become a feminist icon; her focus was on her beliefs and goals. On the other hand, hostile readers in Pakistan (where she has many detractors) probably look at these same qualities and come to precisely *opposite* conclusions – that Malala is rebellious, hypercritical and blasphemous. This illustrates how an audience's context influences their perception and interpretation of a character.

Contradictions

Readers might feel as if incidents or opinions have been placed in the memoir specifically to refute Malala's critics back home; this sometimes introduces tensions between the various ways in which she portrays her own character. For example, she dismisses the many awards she won before the assassination attempt (and their significant prize money) as 'jewels without much meaning' (p.181). This forms an incongruous contrast with the image of the girl who continues to obsess about winning the top academic prize in her small class. Malala can be very self-effacing – for example, she states that 'any of the girls in my class could have achieved what I had achieved if they had had their parents' support' (p.181). While undercutting the extraordinary level of personal courage she obviously possesses, this also downplays an ambitiousness never explicitly stated but everywhere apparent in this memoir. Malala is not afraid to criticise Pakistan's leaders or the Taliban, but at times she is cautious about articulating her own motivations. She clearly wants to turn an oppressive system on its head, but she doesn't want to be seen to be defying the codes under which she was raised: 'I was a good girl. In my heart I had only the desire to help people. It wasn't about the awards or the money' (p.254).

Although Malala is undeniably a champion of women's rights, she distances herself to some extent from some of the basic tenets of Western feminism. She is proud of her father for celebrating the birth of a daughter, but then seems equally proud of his reason for doing so: 'I know there is something different about this child' (p.9). It could be argued that celebrating someone for being 'different' from a repressive stereotype only serves to reinforce it. While Malala encourages her readers to celebrate Ziauddin when he insists that he will protect her freedom (p.55), at this point she does not criticise the system in which women can't achieve even the most basic freedoms *without* a man's indulgence. Of course, Malala does make protests elsewhere, but her dutifulness to her father and lack of acknowledgement that Ziauddin's intentions may in fact fortify *Pashtunwali* could be considered to undercut her protests.

Another contrast within Malala's character is between her formidable identity as a young activist and her prosaic experience as a normal teenage girl. Despite her beliefs and her political acclaim, she still has regular conversations with Moniba about the *Twilight* series and Justin Bieber songs (p.4).

Her time in the Birmingham hospital gives us an insight into Malala's responses to some Western values, despite the fact that other Western values are in line with her beliefs about rights. She is so offended by seeing girls training in their sports bras in *Bend it Like Beckham* that she makes the nurses turn it off. They had, of course, chosen the film because they expected Malala to like something about 'a Sikh girl challenging her cultural norms' (p.242). As a result they give her cartoons to watch instead. The only way for the staff to be certain of not upsetting her is to treat Malala like a young child, quarantining this political activist and deep thinker from all the engaging ideas that might inadvertently accompany material too 'offensive' for her.

Family

It's common for childhood memoirs to focus on parents as much as the child herself. Malala pays tribute many times to her mother, but these tributes are oddly impersonal. Though she spends much more time with Malala than Ziauddin does, Toor Pekai disappears from the memoir for significant patches. This may reflect Malala's relationship with her mother, or (as discussed on p.15 of this guide) it might reflect her mother's position in society: a dedicated observer of purdah, Toor Pekai is a deeply private woman and may not have wanted the memoir to reveal much about her. Malala recognises the 'great sacrifice' Toor Pekai makes, and how 'very difficult' it must have been for her when, on Malala's sixteenth birthday, she allows herself 'to be publicly photographed for the first time' (p.262). Malala deeply respects her mother, but does not seem to share many of her interests.

Malala is much more like Ziauddin, whom she idolises. She shares his courage in the face of danger and his commitment to political and ethical causes; both of them see their activism as a matter in which they really have no choice. The idea of giving in to their oppressors never seems to enter their minds. Given the nature of these opposing forces, Malala's and Ziauddin's refusal to capitulate appears to be such a great strength that readers may not stop to consider the inverse implication: extreme inflexibility. We see it in Malala's competitiveness at school, her constant bickering with Moniba and Khushal, and even in an episode that otherwise reflects well on her: she so repudiates her period of stealing when she was seven that she vows never again to wear jewellery. This response seems extreme, just as her 'crime' – stealing item after item from Safina – was a disproportionate response to the younger girl's possible theft of a single toy.

Ziauddin has given Malala her love of education; it is portrayed almost as a physical need in her. Both of them feel very comfortable in front of an audience making speeches (despite Ziauddin's early challenges posed by his stutter), and seem to relish the opportunity to do so. Each of them is very concerned about the environment; Malala's love of the natural beauty of her valley is particularly notable.

Faith and devotion

The book leaves no doubt about the strength of Malala's commitment to Islam and God. She includes many of her prayers and ends the book with a reassertion of her reliance on God. Malala's faith seems to be behind one of the most interesting developments in her character: her refusal to hate the men who ordered or carried out the attempt on her life. As she says elsewhere, 'when you see death, things change' (p.246). The Malala who writes from Birmingham seems dramatically different from the one she reflects on in Swat. Though still very young, the course of her life has been set; she intends to devote the rest of it to the cause of education, for both girls and boys who are being denied it.

If the pre-shooting Malala was reactive in her activism – standing up for her rights against fundamentalists – the later Malala seems both more serene and expansive. This is may be the result of her broadened perspective on the world, as opposed to her more restricted focus on her own struggles and those of her small community before she had ever left the Swat Valley. This is suggested in Malala's assertion at the end of the book that the 'girl who was shot by the Taliban' feels like someone else. The girl who used to model herself on fiercely combative figures like Alexander the Great and Malalai of Maiwand has come through an episode of extreme personal violence to embrace nonviolent resistance and activism. If nothing else, the capacity for personal growth should indicate that there is never a single answer to the question, 'who is Malala?' or who, for that matter, anyone is.

Ziauddin Yousafzai

Key quotes

'He found himself torn between the two extremes, secularism and socialism on one side and militant Islam on the other. I guess he ended up somewhere in the middle.' (p.28)

'... when Ziauddin is in a crisis he becomes strong and his spirits high.' (Hidayatullah, p.41)

'They wanted to kill two birds with one stone. Kill Malala and silence me for ever.' (Ziauddin, p.208)

I Am Malala is as much about Ziauddin as it is about his daughter. Even when the book is not specifically following his activities (independent of his daughter), Ziauddin can always be counted on as the source for an apposite quote for any situation. Malala says that her father was 'out a lot as he was busy' (p.17), yet his presence hovers over every aspect of her life. It's pertinent here to consider, again, elements of the book's genesis and construction. Christina Lamb would have relied primarily on interviews with its principals to construct her narrative; one gets the impression that Ziauddin had a lot to say about many things.

Key point

Ziauddin's dominating presence introduces a paradox: Malala, in fighting for women's rights to independence, acknowledges that without her father's progressive attitudes she would never have been able to speak up for these rights.

It could be argued that Ziauddin is too active in his daughter's life (and, correspondingly, too present in her memoir), yet it can also be argued that he is a heroic figure. He scratches his way to a prominent place in a stratified society from the most meagre beginnings. His life is a series of fights for important causes (for example, the environment and the rights of Pashtuns), but his driving passion is education. Ziauddin believes that both boys and girls are entitled to an education based on independent thought, open-mindedness and creativity, rather than obedience (pp.37–8). He resists the prejudices and pressures of his culture and speaks out fearlessly for what he believes, even going into Fazlullah's village to speak his mind (p.104).

The arguments he makes against the Taliban are sensible; but lacking the platform that a government official or a khan (as a descendant of the traditional ruling class in Pakistan) might have, Ziauddin is not heeded. This changes somewhat when the media, first Pakistani and then international, start paying attention to the plight of educators under the Taliban. Nevertheless, Ziauddin's platform remains small until Malala herself becomes involved. It is the short film made about her for the *New York Times* (Chapter 13) that really brings attention to the family.

In the end, the most important things about Ziauddin are his dedication to education, his intelligent assessments of the situation in Swat and Pakistan, his astounding courage and his staunch support for his daughter. Yet we can't overlook the effects his activism has on his family. For example, when the family flees the valley before the military assault against the Taliban (Chapter 15), Ziauddin's decision to leave the others after the first night seems reckless. His willingness to die for his beliefs is admirable, but who would support the family if he were killed? The text has revealed only too vividly the lack of both women's and widows' rights in the *Pashtunwali* code; it is implausible to imagine Toor Pekai taking over the Khushal School.

Toor Pekai

Key quotes

'Though my mother was not educated, she was the practical one in the family, the doer while my father was the talker. She was always out helping people … Wherever we lived my mother filled our house with people.' (p.66)

'In our house my mother managed everything because my father was so busy.' (p.95)

Malala's mother can neither read nor write. She is very devout, praying five times a day at home (women are not allowed in mosques – see p.17). Toor Pekai is often out visiting people in hospital or taking food to those in need, and the house is always full of less fortunate relatives or students from the school with nowhere else to live. When, at the end of the book, the family is in exile in Birmingham, it is she who seems to be suffering the most in her (relatively) empty house.

Toor Pekai embodies much in the *Pashtunwali* code besides the obligation of hospitality. She believes firmly in purdah, telling Malala that she should be veiled when she is giving interviews on television. Her husband reassures her that purdah 'is not only in the veil, purdah is in the heart' (p.96). She is brave and resourceful when it comes to getting the family to Shangla, including using her shoe to beat a man who comes too close to her (p.151). But it is notable that upon learning that Malala has been shot Toor Pekai does not rush to the hospital; she goes home to pray.

Unlike Ziauddin's presence in *I Am Malala*, Toor Pekai's is somewhat sketchy. Everything we learn about her seems to come filtered first through Ziauddin or Malala's observations – and their judgements.

Madam Maryam

Key quotes

> 'Madam Maryam had even got married so she could stay in Swat. Her family had moved to Karachi to get away from the conflict and, as a woman, she could not live alone.' (p.133)
>
> 'We were lucky too that Madam Maryam was brave and resisted the pressure to stop working ... "The secret school is our silent protest," she told us.' (p.139)

Madam Maryam is the headmistress at Ziauddin's school. Ziauddin has known Maryam since she was ten, and she seems to be the most trusted member of his staff. Among other things, she signals to him to wind up his speeches when he has been talking too long. She is obviously as dedicated as he is to education. She is a conspirator in the plan to let the older girls – Malala and her classmates – pretend to be in primary school when the Taliban forbids education beyond those years: an act of resistance that could have resulted in them all being killed (Chapter 14).

Madam Maryam is a kind of surrogate mother for Malala, a mother outside the home. We see this most clearly when Malala is shot and Toor Pekai remains at home to pray; it is Madam Maryam who rushes to the hospital on the back of her husband's motorbike – a mode of transport not quite respectable. Once there, Maryam pretends to be Malala's mother so that she will be allowed to stay by her side and help Ziauddin make decisions about his daughter's care.

Baba

Key quotes

> 'My grandfather would rail against the class system, the continuing power of the khans and the gap between the haves and have-nots.' (p.23)
>
> '*Baba* also gave him [Ziauddin] a deep love of learning and knowledge as well as a keen awareness of people's rights, which my father has passed on to me.' (p.30)

Malala's paternal grandfather, Rohul Amim, plays a significant role in the early part of the book but then mostly fades from it. A very difficult man, known for his rages and his grudges, he is important primarily as a stumbling block for Ziauddin. An imam and teacher known for his speeches, *Baba* ridicules his son's stammer. Ziauddin's triumph at public speaking (p.31) demonstrates his ability to overcome paternal adversity as it foreshadows Malala's later renown and bravery as a speaker. Though his relations with *Baba* are obviously strained, Ziauddin honours his father for giving him 'the most important gift – the gift of education' (p.30).

Maulana Fazlullah

Key quotes

'He introduced himself as an Islamic reformer and an interpreter of the Quran.' (p.92)

'... this so-called scholar is spreading ignorance.' (Ziauddin, p.94)

Fazlullah is the leader of the Taliban in the Swat Valley, where he begins accumulating followers through his daily pirate-radio broadcasts. At first even Toor Pekai enjoys his recommendations about good Muslim practice. Many enjoy the gossipy way Fazlullah singles out individuals for incorrect observance or congratulates those who give up sinful ways. Soon the community is supporting him with donations of cash and gold and free labour to build a large compound including a mosque and *madrasa* (p.96). Fazlullah then sets up a *shura,* an Islamic court, and adjudicates cases; his men start going into the community itself to police behaviour deemed as immodest or un-Islamic. Very soon, the people of Swat are living under a repressive theocratic (ruled according to religious principles) police state. Whippings and threats become beheadings and massacres, with bodies dumped frequently in one of Mingora's main squares. Cultural artefacts are destroyed and a crippling uniformity is forced upon the people (p.103).

The Taliban is much bigger than one man; despite his control in the valley, his power is not infinite. His real role is to lure the Pashtuns of Swat, through charisma and the promise of guidance towards a devout life, into loyalty to the extremist organisation. The text suggests that Fazlullah found and took advantage of a community ripe and ready for Talibanisation (see 'Themes, ideas & values').

THEMES, IDEAS & VALUES

The rights of women

Key quotes

> 'It was as though they wanted to remove all traces of womankind from public life.' (p.80)
>
> '... the fact was that we were a country where almost all the women depend entirely on men.' (p.183)

The previous section of this guide touched on Malala's dutifulness – to her father, to her traditions and to Islam – positing the possibility that her desire to be seen as 'a good girl' (p.254), acting only in accord with the better principles of her homeland, is intended to defuse accusations of radicalness, or of feminism as we know it in the West. Malala comments most directly on the issue of women's rights at the beginning of Chapter 18.

> I sat on the rocks and thought about the fact that across the water were lands where women were free. In Pakistan we had had a woman prime minister and in Islamabad I had met those impressive working women, yet the fact was that we were a country where almost all the women depend entirely on men (p.183).

Then, in a rather poetic passage, Ziauddin asks Malala what she is 'dreaming about' (p.184). Her answer, 'Just about crossing oceans, *Aba'* (p.184), is, of course, intended to have a double meaning. Malala does not want merely to travel to countries where women are more free than in Pakistan; she dreams too of a freer Pakistan, but knows that her country is 'oceans' away from allowing women the rights they've won in the West. Getting there will entail a long and dangerous voyage.

One can sympathise with Malala; talking about these subjects is fraught with danger and misunderstanding. Her reputation among Islamic conservatives at home is as a Westernising radical. Opinions and actions in this book – things Western readers might not see as controversial – undoubtedly inflame those readers. Yet her protests and solutions to the oppression of women in Pakistan might, on the other hand, seem too weak to satisfy some Western readers. In between the two passages just quoted, she writes,

> In Pakistan when women say they want independence, people think this means we don't want to obey our fathers, brothers or husbands. But it does not mean that. It means we want to make decisions for ourselves (p.183).

This sounds reasonable but the question naturally arising from it is: what do you do when your father, brother or husband forbids you to make decisions for yourself? It is impossible to be both autonomous *and* obedient.

The *Pashtunwali* code as Malala describes it is essentially an entire culture of men forbidding women autonomy. The book is rife with examples of women caught 'making decisions for themselves' (even minor ones) and paying for it with their lives: Shabana murdered for being a dancer (pp.123–4); Seema, murdered for flirting with a boy (p.54); the two sisters murdered for dancing in public (p.264). Only the killing of Shabana was carried out by the Taliban; the others were murdered by their own families. In the West, history has shown that if women want to be free they have to be willing to disobey their fathers and brothers and husbands.

I Am Malala does a service to women's rights by bringing to a wide audience such cases of violence, along with its many examples of other forms of sexist oppression in Swat and Pakistan. But, despite her bravery in standing up for her beliefs, Malala seems ever to be restraining herself from saying too much. Even when it comes to the women who so impressed her in Islamabad, the 'lawyers and doctors and also activists', Malala qualifies both her admiration and their example: it 'showed us that women could do important jobs yet still keep their culture and traditions' (p.162). Her comment echoes the situation of Madam Maryam, compelled to marry so she can remain in Swat after her family leaves (p.133). This suggests that, to do an important job, women must accept compromise in the form of obligation to the more restrictive elements of culture and tradition.

The above quote from page 162 encapsulates one of Malala's central missions and thus a central theme of the book: gaining acceptance for improved women's rights – but only with minimal disturbance to cultural values. By contrast, Western feminism aims to change cultures by challenging sexism wherever it occurs within them. Taking Malala's description of the *Pashtunwali* code as our guide, one can only conclude that it is fundamentally sexist. This highlights a deep tension in Malala's fight and in the book, an unanswered question inherent in trying to emancipate Pashtun women without destroying the code that entraps them. Malala's words on page 54 clearly articulate this tension:

> I am very proud to be a Pashtun but sometimes I think our code of conduct has a lot to answer for, particularly where the treatment of women is concerned.

Other forms of power

Malala writes,

> Our men think earning money and ordering around others is where power lies. They don't think power is in the hands of the woman who takes care of everyone all day long, and gives birth to their children. (p.95)

An example of this form of female power is Malala's own mother, who takes care of all the housework in Swat and teaches the children 'how to behave' (p.95). Due to Ziauddin's frequent absences, Toor Pekai must also take on responsibilities normally reserved for men, like taking the children to the hospital for operations. Contravening purdah in this way makes her uncomfortable, but Ziauddin assures her that 'purdah is not only in the veil, purdah is in the heart' (p.96).

Malala identifies the fact that there are different sources of power operating in a society and in a home, but her words don't really challenge the *dynamics* of this power. If it is true that the men 'don't think power is in the hands' of women who run households, it is also true that they are never challenged to consider an alternative. *Pashtunwali* dictates total subservience of women to men, and purdah demands that women stay in the home. The text shows that there are few willing to challenge men's assumptions and beliefs in this religious and cultural tenet. While Malala's work and writing dignify the role of the oppressed, this does not always equate to challenging the power structures that keep them that way. Her words are a form of protest, but she does not acknowledge that the powerful work women do in the home is not a result of strong choice: it is because they are prohibited from virtually any other work.

That Ziauddin allows his wife to do things normally forbidden to women speaks to a progressiveness on his part (although these decisions do also suit his own convenience). Yet, as with the reasons he gives for honouring his baby girl (because she is 'different', p.9), his advice to Toor Pekai sometimes reinforces the power imbalance. He is not suggesting that his wife liberate herself from the idea of purdah; Ziauddin is merely suggesting that she keep herself bound to it in a way that transcends place. Whether she observes purdah in the veil or in the heart, it is still a form of captivity.

Education

Key quotes

'Going to school, reading and doing our homework wasn't just a way of passing time, it was our future.' (p.122)

'Education is neither Eastern nor Western, it is human.' (p.136)

On the subject of education, Malala makes compelling points; writing from the heart, she also writes as though on safer ground than when she addresses the gendered power imbalance. Most Pashtun women do not have access to an education; they rarely even learn to read or write, but there isn't anything in the *Pashtunwali* code or in the Quran that says they may not go to school. It is only when the Taliban come that a total ban is imminent. Of course, the Taliban's ideas are extensions of *Pashtunwali*. Where the code merely discourages, the Taliban explicitly forbid.

Why is it that so few Pashtun girls go to school? Toor Pekai's own case sums it up well. Though bright, she dropped out after less than a single term: 'there seemed no point in going to school just to end up cooking, cleaning and bringing up children' (p.32). An education is wasted on one who is valued little beyond reproduction and manual servitude – even at six, Malala's mother could see this. What she would not have understood is how threatening the education of girls is to those with an interest in keeping them in servitude. It will fall to her daughter Malala to learn this lesson.

Education is Ziauddin's life's work. He builds up his school from meagre beginnings, promoting creativity and independent thought (pp.38–9), a philosophy in direct contrast to the *madrasa* system, which inculcates its students with an unquestioning and bigoted religious fundamentalism. Perhaps part of the reason Malala feels on safer ground expressing herself on education is that, unlike with the subject of purdah and women's rights, Malala's parents are unambiguously on the side of increased access and liberality in education. There isn't the sense that Malala is being overly cautious, holding back from expressing notions of which her parents might not quite approve. Her ideas about education originate in Ziauddin's philosophy, and her resultant commitment to girls' rights to education is as strong as his.

Malala portrays herself as always loving school and being quite competitive about grades. But it is only when the Taliban threaten to take it all away that she realises how central education is to her life: 'going to school, reading and doing our homework wasn't just a way of passing time, it was our future' (p.122).

As impassioned as she is on the subject, Malala is careful to refute the Taliban on *their* terms. Against the Taliban's claim that they are defending Islam, she argues that:

> Islam has given us this right [to education] and says that every girl and boy should go to school. The Quran says we should seek knowledge, study hard and learn the mysteries of our world. (p.129)

After Malala is shot, the Taliban use as their justification that she was 'promoting Western culture in Pashtun areas' (p.216). However, earlier in the book, Malala has asserted that 'Education is neither Eastern nor Western, it is human' (p.136).

At the end of *I Am Malala*, convinced that God has preserved her life for a purpose, Malala dedicates the rest of it to working for the right of children to be educated. Her very experiences have been quite an education, but she still has a long way to go: 'I want to learn and be trained well with the weapon of knowledge. Then I will be able to fight more effectively for my cause' (p.263). It is interesting that Malala uses metaphors of war to describe education – the group that targeted her for assassination, the Taliban, sees education purely in terms of conflict. The severely proscribed education given to males in *madrasas* in Pakistan and elsewhere – an education divorcing them from their family and promoting zealotry – has become primarily focused on creating unthinking fighters and martyrs.

It is easy to understand why a 'Western' or 'liberal' education (particularly for girls) would be seen as such a threat within this climate. The Taliban rarely use women as fighters. Girls do not necessarily receive the same level of brainwashing boys' *madrasas* often provide; and any other kind of education might prompt them to question the total oppression – physical, spiritual, mental and sexual – the Taliban has reserved for women. Ziauddin talks elsewhere about a 'purdah of the heart'. What the Taliban are trying to achieve by banning education for girls is a purdah of the mind.

Talibanisation

Key quotes

'It seemed that people had decided the Taliban were here to stay and they had better get along with them.' (p.125)

'We people of Swat were first seduced by the Taliban, then killed by them and now blamed for them.' (p.159)

'The Taliban is ... a mentality, and this mentality is everywhere in Pakistan.' (p.194)

While the Taliban was created by Pashtun men and much of its ideology is founded on *Pashtunwali*, this is not to suggest that the Taliban and the Pashtuns are equivalent. The very brutality the Taliban resorted to against the Pashtun people of Swat indicates how differently *they* saw themselves from their brethren.

But the question remains: was the link between *Pashtunwali* and the religious extremists part of why the Yousafzais' fellow Swatis were so easily taken in by the Taliban? The organisation and what it represented were not unknown; when Fazlullah began his broadcasts in late 2007, the group had already been in existence for more than a decade in neighbouring Afghanistan, and had become a world pariah after the 9/11 attacks in the US. More than ten thousand Swatis went to fight NATO alongside the Taliban in 2002 (p.71). There could have been no surprise about the extremes of their ideology or their violence. Yet even Toor Pekai, married to a man who stands for everything the Taliban hate, is receptive to Fazlullah's broadcasts at first (p.92). A little gossip, a little advice about Islamic ritual, some ranting against the government in Islamabad – everyone seems to have found something to like. Malala suggests that her people were in a kind of trance (p.103); Ziauddin says that they were 'seduced' (p.159).

Of course, Malala and Ziauddin give plenty of other reasons why the Taliban were able to gain a foothold. People whose disputes are dragged out in corrupt civil courts welcome the Taliban's promise of bringing swift resolutions through a local *shura* (court, p.98). That it might be discriminatory, in a way the Pakistani civil law is not, doesn't seem to bother anyone; as the text shows, this is a people whose code of ethics calls for vigilantism and revenge (p.59). When Fazlullah forbids women to go to the Cheena Bazaar, many men are happy because it saves them money (p.99). In a place where women are so oppressed, it is unsurprising that further erosion of women's rights is viewed by men only in terms of how their own lives will be affected.

Another explanation offered for the lure of the Taliban relates to class. Malala says that many manual workers, labouring in a society that does not respect them, joined the Taliban 'to finally achieve status and power' (p.124). It should be remembered that Fazlullah was a poorly educated former operator of a pulley chair to cross the river, and his deputy, Shah Douran, used to sell snacks in the bazaar (p.92). Additionally, many of the women who are moved to donate their jewellery or money to Fazlullah come from 'poor villages or households where the husbands were working abroad' (p.96) – that is, in addition to being women, they are further disadvantaged by economic stratification. Fazlullah's preaching against the khans positions him as a kind of Robin Hood figure (p.94); Malala says that 'poor people were happy to see the khans getting their comeuppance' (p.94). However, the khans hold themselves above everyone not born to their status, so it is not only the resentment of the poor that is being stoked; Fazlullah is also trying to get the middle and professional classes on his side.

A final reason given for the Swatis' acceptance of the Taliban is rather surprising. Malala writes,

> Our people are used to being subservient because under the wali no criticism was tolerated. If anyone offended him, their entire family could be expelled from Swat. (p.62)

The wali was the leader of Swat during the period when the valley had a level of autonomy under British colonisation; but the highest authority in Swat now is the deputy commissioner (DC), sent from Islamabad. Once the Taliban make enough inroads into Swat to get the DC on their side, the people fully accept the organisation. As Malala observes, 'We say in Arabic, "People follow their king." When the highest authority in your district joins the Taliban, then Talibanisation becomes normal' (p.126). This is one of the first instances in the book of the word Talibanisation. About the notion of Talibanisation, Ziauddin's old friend Hidayatullah has this to say: 'the Taliban is not an organised force like we imagine ... It's a mentality, and this mentality is everywhere in Pakistan' (p.194).

Although Hidayatullah is not speaking specifically about Swat here, his words help to supply an answer to the question of how the Talibanisation of Swat occurred so easily. It is Hidayatullah who, earlier in the book, warns Ziauddin about how the Taliban would proceed in Swat:

> They want to win the hearts and minds of the people so they first see what the local problems are and target those responsible, and that way they get the support of the silent majority. (p.94)

After the Taliban have been exposed and defeated by the army, Ziauddin sums up the relationship this way: 'we people of Swat were first seduced by the Taliban, then killed by them and now blamed for them. Seduced, killed and blamed' (p.159). There is no question that the Swatis were seduced by the Taliban, although this explanation does not account for the active role that some men and women in Swat played.

Once the Taliban are forced to release their grip on the whole of Swat a much worse personal threat occurs: the targeting of those who speak out. The book calls this a private Talibanisation (Chapter 19), but it is not so different from the beginning of the Taliban's campaign, when they targeted people on the fringes – such as the dancer Shabana – people whom the majority of Swatis were not willing to defend ('people loved to see Shabana dance but didn't respect her, and when she was murdered they said nothing', p.124). As in the Martin Niemöller poem that Ziauddin keeps in his pocket (p.116), now the Taliban are coming for *them*. We know the results: Malala is shot and the family has to flee

Pakistan. Talibanisation is not just the seduction of a population; it is also a method of eliminating problematic and vulnerable segments of that population. In this, the text suggests that the broader population is often complicit.

Activism and altruism

Key quotes

'Wherever we lived my mother filled the house with people' (p.66).

'I was speaking up for my rights as a Muslim woman to be able to go to school.' (p.238)

'I was spared for a reason – to use my life for helping people.' (p.255)

Malala and Ziauddin are both activists for education. That means they speak out wherever they can against the Taliban's plans to forbid girls from going to school. They strategise, they organise, they campaign, they demonstrate. Activism is a public activity whose most potent weapon is exposure. It requires an audience. Altruism is acting for the benefit of others, either publicly or privately. It begins with a consciousness, not of offence but of beneficence. Altruism is sometimes called other-person-centredness (the opposite of self-centredness). It is not merely doing things for others; it is a state of mind in which doing things for others is paramount among many competing values.

While the two philosophies differ, they are not mutually exclusive or even in opposition to each other. Sometimes the best way to do good is to publicly expose unfairness. There can be little doubt that Malala is sincere in her desire to help children throughout the world to get a better education. But she comes most prominently to activism – from a more general feeling of wanting to good in the world – only when something she loves (her education) is threatened.

By contrast, Ziauddin seems to be an activist from the start. Before fighting for education rights, he was an activist for Pashtun rights (p.36) and for the environment (pp.68–9). He is a man who loves to argue and debate, someone with strong progressive ideals in a conservative country. And, like his daughter, he possesses great personal courage. Interestingly, Ziauddin is also sought after as a mediator of disputes. Despite his passion, which has been known to cloud judgement, he is obviously seen as impartial and prudent.

The model of altruism in the book is Toor Pekai: 'wherever we lived my mother filled the house with people' (p.66). Consider how casually Malala mentions sharing her bedroom with other girls: Aneesa, Shehnaz, Nooria and Alishpa (pp.66–7). Of course, hospitality is a strong requirement in the *Pashtunwali* code. Ziauddin's powerlessness to refuse taking in the distant family members who descend the moment he opens his first school costs him his business partner (p.39). But Toor Pekai's altruism goes beyond what is required. More importantly, it seems to be a defining feature of her character. It is personal and limited to the private sphere.

There is a transition in the book's protagonist, from her mother's kind of altruism to her father's activism. As a young child praying to God to help her make the world perfect (p.72), Malala is filled with a general desire to do good. Her encounter with the girl of the rubbish mountain (Chapter 6) instils a need to do a specific good; imploring her father to give the children free places at the school is specifically altruistic. Later, when the Taliban threaten to end her education, Malala becomes an activist: she folds her personal dilemma into a shared wrong and brings it to national and then international attention. After she has been shot, evacuated and resettled, Malala undergoes another shift. No longer personally threatened, she vows to continue her activism using her fame as a platform. But now she is not just doing it for herself and Moniba and the other girls from the Khushal School. Her activism is beginning to resemble her childhood prayers, as though she's come full circle: the world itself will be her arena, but she will try to improve it through the specific area of her expertise.

As a work of fact rather than fiction, *I Am Malala* is somewhat bound by the complexities of real life, and the separation between the two philosophies is not a clean one. Ziauddin's altruism in providing so many free places at his school and in mediating disputes seems to be detached from his activism (p.67). Toor Pekai's altruism is limited to the personal sphere, but if she were not restricted by purdah, she might well become a more public activist. (The text hints at this when, after Malala's shooting, her parents are not able to travel to Birmingham so Toor Pekai threatens a hunger strike in protest, p.239.) It should be remembered, too, that activism is not limited to those fighting for equality or freedom. The Taliban are activists for their 'purer' form of Islam and a return to sharia law. Consider the girls of the Red Mosque (pp.105–6), terrorising Islamabad in the name of the extremist views they've learned at school. Like Malala, they are ready to die for their cause, but they are activists devoid of altruism. More complicated are groups such as Jamaat-ul-Dawa, the charity wing of a terrorist organisation. After the earthquake the group saves lives in Swat by getting medical supplies, food and shelter to victims (p.87). While on one level this behaviour is altruistic, it is also tempered by the uses to which the organisation intends to put the resulting goodwill.

DIFFERENT INTERPRETATIONS

Different interpretations arise from different responses to a text. Over time, a text will evoke a wide range of responses from its readers, who may come from various social or cultural groups and live in very different places and historical periods. Responses by critics and reviewers can be published in newspapers, journals and books, both online and in print. They can also be expressed in discussions among readers in the media, classrooms, book groups and so on.

While there is no single correct reading or interpretation of a text, it is important to understand that an interpretation is more than a personal opinion – it is the justification of a point of view on the text. To present an interpretation of a text based on your point of view, you must use a logical argument and support it with relevant evidence from the text.

The critics' viewpoints

Published late in 2013, *I Am Malala* is a relatively recent text, and as such there have been limited developments in critical attitudes beyond the initial reviews. Malala herself has remained active and in the public view, giving interviews. As she undergoes changes in outlook and opinion, *I Am Malala* will become increasingly less relevant both to her story and, perhaps, to her political and cultural impact. One reviewer, Marie Arana of the *Washington Post* (2013), likens Malala to an Anne Frank 'who lived'. Anne Frank's diary is sadly all that remains of its subject. As such it has attracted a lot of critical attention; there is simply nowhere else to go but the text itself to understand Anne, an extremely sympathetic young woman doomed to a horrific fate. Malala is also very sympathetic, but as a survivor of her fate, she retains agency, the ability to speak for herself beyond the confines of her text.

An interesting potential critic of the book is Malala herself, as she reflects back on it with increasing distance. *I Am Malala* came from a teenager blindsided by traumatic events uprooting her from her home and relocating her in an intimidating foreign country. As she settles into life in the West, and as her education continues, she may well grow away from the traditional values that so guided the memoir. In a 2018 interview with David Letterman (*My Next Guest Needs No Introduction* 2018), she expressed some views that contrast with her earlier views in the book: she no longer wants to be the Prime Minister of Pakistan someday, or any kind of a politician; and, though she was reluctant to call herself one in the past, she now embraces the label of feminist.

While reviews of the book are largely positive (which might be influenced by the recency of the tragic events, and the pre-eminence of its author/subject), some reviews say little about the book itself, using it instead as a starting place to discuss the dire issues facing Pakistan circa 2013. Fatima Bhutto in *The Guardian* (2013) pointed out that there are noticeable differences in the style of writing in different sections of *I Am Malala*. Where Malala is speaking in her own voice it has a 'purity' but where it is obviously Christina Lamb filling in details about history or geography, it is 'stiff'. Other than that, *I Am Malala* has received significant if undetailed praise.

In 2015 it was banned in Pakistani private schools – more than 70 000 schools – by the All Pakistan Private Schools Federation (APPSF). As predictable as this may have been, it must have hurt Ziauddin, a principal himself who had built from nothing a successful school – the kind where a book like *I Am Malala* might even have been assigned reading. The fact that authorities have forbidden students to read the book in some countries and required them to study it in others is a reminder of how deeply an audience's context influences their interpretation of a text.

Two interpretations

Interpretation 1

I Am Malala *is about a young woman who uses the issue of education to challenge the traditions and biases of her country, for the advancement of women.*

This interpretation sees the memoir as a battle cry against the extremely conservative status quo – in law, in custom, in religious freedom, in opportunity – of women's rights in Pakistan. Malala is constantly raising the issue of extreme bias, particularly among the Pashtuns. We learn of young girls being sold as wives to old men against their will, of girls killed by their families merely for flirting or dancing in public. Girls are used to settle disputes among feuding families, as if they were objects and not people. Malala's condemnation does not need to be overt in order to register her disgust. The crimes speak for themselves. The fact that she writes about them indicates her position; if she were only interested in education, she would never talk about these matters.

At the same time, we must not expect Malala to write or behave like a Western feminist. Would she be able to get anyone to heed her in a country where women have so few forums for discussion? Words mean nothing if no-one will listen to them. This is one reason why she follows the strategy of speaking out most strongly about education. To begin with, it is her area of expertise, being a student herself and the daughter of a school founder and principal. It is also something that affects her personally: no-one can accuse her of becoming embedded in arguments she doesn't understand. Additionally, Malala knows that her beliefs have strong foundations when it comes to education. Pakistan's laws say that children are entitled to an education. Perhaps more importantly, she cites examples from the Quran assuring the right to education.

It is very shrewd of her to refute the Taliban's weak arguments against education for girls. This is the most devastating way to confront the group, with reason and precedent. It's also consistent with her pragmatic approach. Her very engagement with the Taliban, and her refusal to stoop to their level of aggression, is a powerful strategy in her fight, and a compelling quality for the protagonist in a narrative. The text shows just how great a threat the Taliban believed Malala to be. They tried to silence her with three bullets; in fact, they only gave her a much broader audience. More than two million copies of her book have been sold, and it has undoubtedly had many more readers.

When she writes about the atrocities committed against women, or how girls are brainwashed into terrorism in the Red Mosque, she communicates forcefully how bad things can be in Pakistan. On the other hand, when she mentions the professional women she saw in Islamabad, Malala gives her readers hope that the nation is not a lost cause. Most importantly, when she addresses the rights of girls to an education, Malala is making her strongest statement about the rights of women. It is a message that *I Am Malala* takes beyond Pakistan's borders and to the whole world.

Interpretation 2

I Am Malala *is about a young woman concerned with her own right to receive an education but unwilling to seriously challenge the traditions and biases against women in her country.*

This interpretation does not question Malala's commitment to her main issue – the right of girls to an education – but sees her as weak and accommodating on other issues to do with women's rights. The fact that Malala raises examples of atrocities committed against girls and women in the Pashtun culture does not demonstrate that she is willing to fight this behaviour. The most she is willing to say is that 'sometimes I think our code of conduct has a lot to answer for' (p.54). It's not that Malala is incapable of censure. She has very strong opinions about the corruption of Pakistani politicians, about the double-dealing of the military, and even about the personal hygiene of members of the Taliban. But when it comes to atrocities against women, the tone of the text becomes more detached, simply reporting facts, with little criticism or comment.

Malala also has very little to say about purdah that could be interpreted as negative. There are certainly times when she makes general complaints about women being controlled by men, and about her own desire to be freer, but she never specifically attacks the system itself or the philosophy behind it. She even celebrates the 'power' of women trapped in it, without commenting on the limits of this power. Perhaps this reflects on the youth and loyalty of the author: Malala did not want to offend her mother, a firm adherent to purdah. It also evinces her reluctance to criticise Pashtun culture in any way more forceful than the quote on the previous page of this guide – while she acknowledges that it is imperfect, it is still the culture of which she is a member, indeed a proud, loyal member.

There is no doubting Malala's sincerity in her fight for girls' education, but her decision to fight the Taliban without confronting the belief system that underlies their actions is disempowering and problematic. It only legitimises a position that does not deserve to be part of the dialogue: anyone who espouses total slavery for women, as the Taliban do through their extremist versions of purdah, should be subjected to much deeper and more powerful scrutiny and condemnation than one young girl can bring to bear.

Unfortunately, Malala is still restricted by her own religious and ethnic loyalties when she looks beyond her region. Her admiration for the professional women she sees in Islamabad is tempered by her insistence that these women are still maintaining their culture and traditions. Those looking for a champion who wants to change the culture that puts women into such subservience (these professional women are a miniscule exception to the rule in Pakistan) will not find it in *I Am Malala*. In some ways, the book's protagonist does not succeed in her ambitions and the Taliban can be said to have won. They achieved their goal of ridding Swat of Malala and her father. While the book has many strong statements to make about the damage extremist religion has done to Swat and Pakistan, Malala remains so deeply embedded in her culture that her activism can tackle only the symptoms of oppression and not the cause.

QUESTIONS & ANSWERS

This section focuses on your own analytical writing on the text, and gives you strategies for producing high-quality responses in your coursework and exam essays.

Essay writing – an overview

An essay on a literary work is a formal and serious piece of writing that presents your point of view on the text, usually in response to a given topic. Your 'point of view' in an essay is your interpretation of the meaning of the text's language, structure, characters, situations and events, supported by detailed analysis of textual evidence.

Analyse – don't summarise

In your essays it is important to avoid simply summarising what happens in a text.

- A **summary** is a description or paraphrase (retelling in different words) of the characters and events. For example: 'Macbeth has a horrifying vision of a dagger dripping with blood before he goes to murder King Duncan.'
- An **analysis** is an explanation of the real meaning or significance that lies 'beneath' the text's words (and images, for a film). For example: 'Macbeth's vision of a bloody dagger shows how deeply uneasy he is about the violent act he is contemplating, and conveys his sense that supernatural forces are impelling him to act.'

A limited amount of summary is sometimes necessary to let your reader know which part of the text you wish to discuss. However, always keep this to a minimum and follow it immediately with your analysis of what this part of the text is really telling us.

Plan your essay

Carefully plan your essay so that you have a clear idea of what you are going to say. The plan ensures that your ideas flow logically, that your argument remains consistent and that you stay on the topic. An essay plan should be a list of **brief dot points** covering no more than half a page.

- Include your central argument or main contention – a concise statement of your overall response to the topic.
- Write three or four dot points for each paragraph, indicating the main idea and evidence/examples from the text. Note that in your essay you will need to *expand* on these points and *analyse* the evidence.

Structure your essay

An essay is a complete, self-contained piece of writing. It has a clear beginning (the introduction), middle (several body paragraphs) and end (the last paragraph or conclusion). It must also have a central argument that runs throughout, linking each paragraph to form a coherent whole. See examples of introductions and conclusions in the 'Analysing a sample topic' and 'Sample answer' sections.

The introduction establishes your overall response to the topic. It includes your main contention and outlines the main evidence you will refer to in the course of the essay. Write your introduction *after* you have done a plan and *before* you write the rest of the essay.

The body paragraphs argue your case – they present evidence from the text and explain how this evidence supports your argument. Each body paragraph needs:

- a strong **topic sentence** (usually the first sentence) that states the main point being made in the paragraph
- **evidence** from the text, including some brief quotations
- **analysis** of the textual evidence, with **explanation** of its significance and how it supports your argument
- **links back to the topic** in one or more statements, usually towards the end of the paragraph.

Connect the body paragraphs so that your discussion flows smoothly. Use some linking words and phrases such as 'similarly' and 'on the other hand', though don't start every paragraph like this. Another strategy is to use a significant word from the last sentence of one paragraph in the first sentence of the next.

Use key terms from the topic – or synonyms for them – throughout, so the relevance of your discussion to the topic is always clear.

The conclusion ties everything together and finishes the essay. It includes strong statements that emphasise your central argument and provide a clear response to the topic.

Avoid simply restating the points made earlier in the essay – this will end on a very flat note and imply that you have run out of ideas and vocabulary. The conclusion should be a logical extension of what you have written, not just a repetition or summary of it. Writing an effective conclusion can be a challenge. Try using these tips:

- Start by linking back to the final sentence of the second-last paragraph – this helps your writing to flow, rather than leaping back to your main contention straight away.
- Use synonyms and expressions with equivalent meanings to vary your vocabulary. This allows you to reinforce your line of argument without being repetitive.
- When planning your essay, think of one or two broad statements or observations about the text's wider meaning. These should be related to the topic and your overall argument. Keep them for the conclusion, since they will give you something 'new' to say but still follow logically from your discussion. The introduction will be focused on the topic, but the conclusion can present a wider view of the text.

Essay topics

1. What impact do Malala's relationships with her parents have on her life?
2. "… I was born a proud daughter of Pakistan, though like all Swatis I thought of myself first as Swati and then Pashtun, before Pakistani." How does Malala's sense of her identity shape her actions?
3. "We should learn everything and then choose which path to follow." Discuss the various beliefs about education presented in the text.
4. "Seduced, killed and blamed." How does the text explain the Taliban's rise to power in Swat?
5. 'Life in Birmingham is as difficult for the Yousafzai family as life under the Taliban.'
   To what extent do you agree?
6. 'Malala both criticises and closely follows the *Pashtunwali* code.' Discuss.
7. "Our men think earning money and ordering around others is where power lies."
   How does the text represent women's power?
8. "The Taliban think we are not Muslims but we are."
   What role does Islam play in the lives of Malala and her parents?
9. Malala calls the Swat Valley "the most beautiful place in all the world" and says that she wants to return. Considering all the terrible things that happen to her and her family there, why do you think this is so?
10. "… any of the girls in my class could have achieved what I had achieved if they had had their parents' support."
    Do you think this is true?

Vocabulary for writing on *I Am Malala*

Epigraph: Often used to describe quotations placed at the beginning of a text but can also be used for quotations preceding sections within a text, as in the *tapey* used in this text.

Madrasa: A school for Islamic religious study.

Memoir: An account of part of the writer's life, often with a focus on social and cultural contexts.

Mullah: An interpreter of the Quran or a man learned in it.

Mufti: A man empowered to rule on Islamic legal questions.

Pashtunwali: The moral code of the Pashtun people.

Purdah: The Islamic cultural practice of the veiling of women and their seclusion from men or strangers.

Taliban: Muslim fundamentalists who banded together during the Afghanistan civil war and later established their movement in Pakistan.

Analysing a sample topic

Malala calls the Swat Valley "the most beautiful place in all the world" and says that she wants to return. Considering all the terrible things that happen to her and her family there, why do you think this is so?

Read the question carefully

You might not come into an exam on *I Am Malala* expecting a topic to include reference to geography. Sometimes unexpected questions can give you a wider range for discussion than those you initially feel more comfortable with. This question uses location as a window into Malala's life in general. It gives you the opportunity to explore many of the *events* in the book ('*the terrible things* that happened to her and her family there'); it gives you a chance to write about a minor *theme* in the book – Malala's appreciation for her homeland ('Malala calls the Swat Valley "the most beautiful place in all the world"'); and it gives you a chance to analyse the text and provide your own opinion ('*why* do *you think* this is so?'). This last part of the question is broadest of all, because it's really about Malala's very identity and character. Remember: when a question has multiple elements, you must address each of the areas (in this case there are three) to get a high mark.

Consider the evidence

Before you start writing, you need to gather your evidence (using scrap paper or a computer), perhaps organising information in clusters or bullet points. Start with the Swat Valley. In Chapter 1 Malala writes about the valley, the 'Switzerland of the East', a place of waterfalls, mountains and wildflowers. Mingora may be crowded and polluted, but even there Malala enjoys looking at the mountains from the roof of her house. At Eid, the family travels up to the mountains to visit extended family; there is some evocative writing about the mountains in Chapter 4.

Next, gather evidence about some of the bad things the family experienced in Swat:

- the earthquake of 2005
- the Taliban's persecution of civilians
- the military's campaign against the Taliban, requiring people to flee
- the destruction of much of the city as a result of the fighting
- the terrible floods not long afterward (made worse by the deforestation under the Taliban)
- the 'private Talibanisation' against the Yousafzais, when the rest of the population was relatively safe
- the attempt to assassinate Malala, and the family's subsequent evacuation to England.

For the last part of the question, you need to do some thinking about Malala's character. Her desire to return is about more than the physical beauty of Swat. It is also because of her attachment to her culture; to the memories of childhood she made there; to the kinds of things she can only do there (such as visit the mountains); to the friends and family left behind. Additionally, you might think about what would be required for return to be possible: Malala would have to be safe from the Taliban.

Devise your contention

Come up with your general contention before writing your introduction. The introduction has two functions: to refer to all parts of the question asked and to set out what your argument will be.

Sample introduction

> Just one of the terrible things that happened to the Yousafzai family in the Swat Valley could fill a memoir. Sadly, there are many, from earthquakes to floods, from the Taliban's reign of terror to the military response, and then, when the region finally seems relatively stable, the attempt on Malala's life that leaves her with a serious head injury. Yet Malala still thinks of Swat as 'the most beautiful place in all the world' and insists that she wants to return. In *I Am Malala*, the protagonist shows that Swat means more to her than beauty. Malala identifies strongly with the customs of her people, the Pashtuns, and with her homeland. She fought for their rights and her own there, friendships and memories were forged. Having been forced away by violence, returning some day would be the ultimate victory over her enemies.

Body paragraph outline

***Body paragraph 1:* the beauty of Swat**

- Briefly discuss some of the physical beauty of Swat and Malala's attachment to it (e.g. 'the Switzerland of the East').
- Mention some of the things she has done that are specific to Swat (e.g. school outings, visiting the Buddha sculptures, sitting on the roof and staring at the mountains).
- Discuss how her life and memories, including school and family life, are tied to this location.

Body paragraph 2: **the terrible things that happened in Swat**

- You should not simply repeat the list of terrible events that you have already included in the introduction. You need to come up with a way of organising them – perhaps by severity.
- You might choose to focus on just a few of the events from the introduction, going into more detail here.
- Though the earthquake and the floods involved much loss of life, the thing that made the deepest impact, both on Swat and the Yousafzais, was the rise of the Taliban. (Provide evidence from the text, such as a quote from Malala, to support this.)

Body paragraph 3: **the Taliban**

- Here you can focus on the complicated story of Malala's family's troubles with the Taliban.
- You should include details of both Malala's and Ziauddin's activism, and the threats resulting from their actions.
- Don't forget to mention the 'private Talibanisation' the Yousafzais are subjected to after the valley has become relatively safe for the rest of the population.

Body paragraph 4: **unfinished business and the need to return**

- The shooting by the Taliban arrested Malala's life in an instant and dramatically changed it in many ways.
- You could look at the 'unfinished business' of her life: the things started but left behind or not completed. This could include friendships, activism, Pashtun traditions and future career.
- This evidence will allow you to respond broadly to the question of why Malala might want to return to a place of trauma. The 'beauty' of Swat for Malala involves more than mere physical beauty.

Sample conclusion

Though it did not kill her, the Taliban's bullet ended Malala's life in Swat. The new one she has made in Birmingham has been dedicated to her cause: the right of every girl and boy in the world to receive an education. But there is more to Malala than that. There are her memories, her friendships, her engagement with local issues and, most importantly, her culture. Everywhere in *I Am Malala*, we find a young woman deeply invested in the life and religion of the Pashtun people. Her story will not be over until she can go back to her homeland. To do so would undo the partial victory the Taliban achieved when they drove Malala away, and it would also be a greater victory for her cause and herself. When she speaks of the beauty of her valley, Malala means so much more than the waterfalls and fields of flowers in Swat.

SAMPLE ANSWER

"The Taliban think we are not Muslims but we are."
What role does Islam play in the lives of Malala and her parents?

'I love my God. I thank my Allah. I talk to him all day.' This is from the last page of *I Am Malala*, but Malala's strong faith is everywhere in the book. As a young child she'd pray for a 'magic pencil' to help the world, or to grow taller; as a teenager she defends her activism for girls' education with the Quran's instructions to 'seek knowledge' and 'learn the mysteries of our world'. Malala's strong faith comes from her parents. Toor Pekai prays five times a day and keeps strict purdah. Ziauddin's school is progressive for Swat, but always within the teachings of Islam. Yet the Taliban accuse the family of not being Muslims; it is one of the tactics they use to sow terror in the population. Anyone not adhering to their fundamentalist interpretations of Islam is labelled 'not Muslim', which in turn justifies their being targeted for murder, as Malala was. What really makes the Taliban afraid of the Yousafzais is their dedication to an Islam open to knowledge, creativity and independent thinking.

Though she cannot read the Quran because she had insufficient education, and is not allowed in the mosque because she is a woman, Toor Pekai observes all the rituals of Islam and is described by her daughter as devout. She embodies Islam's injunction to be charitable by taking needy people into her home. Her illiteracy can be a cause of exasperation to Malala, who is embarrassed that her mother believes the Quran forbids women to go into public if unaccompanied by a male relative. Toor Pekai does not try to stop Malala carrying out her activism, but she tells her daughter to cover her face when she speaks to the media, something Malala will not do. One incident sums up the depth of Toor Pekai's faith and observance: when she hears that her daughter has been shot, she does not try to get to the hospital, as Madam Maryam does; she returns home and gathers a group of women to help her pray for Malala's recovery.

Ziauddin's religious dedication is also strong. When he was in his teens, he flirted with the kind of religious fundamentalism the Taliban would later bring to Swat. But his own father's strong beliefs in class struggle also instilled in him a fervour for socialism. As a man, Ziauddin has thrown himself into many causes, from the rights of Pashtuns in Pakistan and the protection of the environment of Swat to the right of all children to an education. Through it all he maintains his faith. When Mullah Ghulamullah brings a group of elders to chastise him for educating girls, he surpasses the *mufti* in knowledge of the Quran. In response to the men's surprise that there are so many Qurans in his house, Ziauddin declares, 'I am a Muslim'. He tells Malala that 'a mullah who is not fully learned is a danger to faith', and this explains Ziauddin's antagonism towards the Taliban. He and Malala see the Taliban's teachings as a total distortion of Islam; they 'deliberately misinterpret the Quran' to gain power and terrorise people.

The Taliban want total uniformity. Their view of Islam is not merely distorted, it is extremely narrow. They want everyone to act the same, think the same and even dress the same, down to the length of their trousers. But Ziauddin's educational philosophy is based on independent thought and creativity even within a religious framework. As Malala says in one of her interviews, 'we should learn everything and then choose which path to follow'. This is the essence of individuality. A population that knows how to think for itself cannot easily be controlled; thus the Taliban feel deeply threatened by Malala and her father. The Yousafzais encourage pursuing knowledge and interpreting the meaning of the Quran directly from its words, not from the propaganda of ignorant *muftis* who want to close schools.

Malala says about the Taliban, 'we believe in God more than they do and we trust him to protect us.' We see that trust in Toor Pekai's altruism and her prayers when Malala is shot. It is in Ziauddin's insistence that education and independent thought will not lead Muslims away from God but towards God. It is in the courage Malala shows in continuing to speak out against the Taliban after receiving death threats. It is in her interpretation of her survival of the assassination attempt as an offering from God of a kind of rebirth. Her decision to dedicate her 'second life' to education rights is a reaffirmation of her strong faith in a God who answered her prayer to be taller by raising her to a platform to speak for what she believes in. Even her prayer for a magic pen to help the world was answered: she used it to write *I Am Malala*.

REFERENCES & READING

Text

Yousafzai, M and Lamb, C 2013, *I Am Malala*, Weidenfeld & Nicolson, London.

References

Reviews

Arana, M 2013, 'Book review: *I Am Malala* by Malala Yousafzai', *Washington Post*, 11 October, https://www.washingtonpost.com/opinions/book-review-i-am-malala-by-malala-yousafzai/2013/10/11/530ba90a-329a-11e3-9c68-1cf643210300_story.html?noredirect=on&utm_term=.03c0da5cb821

Bhutto, F 2013, '*I Am Malala* by Malala Yousafzai: review', *The Guardian*, 30 October, https://www.theguardian.com/books/2013/oct/30/malala-yousafzai-fatima-bhutto-review

Garton, R 2013, '*I Am Malala*: A Book Review', *Albert Shanker Institute*, 12 November, http://www.shankerinstitute.org/blog/i-am-malala-book-review

Roberts, Y 2013, '*I Am Malala* by Malala Yousafzai: review', *The Guardian*, 13 October, https://www.theguardian.com/books/2013/oct/13/malala-yousafzai-biography-taliban

Warsi, S 2013, 'Baroness Warsi: Malala has turned a tragedy into something positive', *Telegraph*, 8 October, https://www.telegraph.co.uk/culture/books/bookreviews/10364317/Baroness-Warsi-Malala-has-turned-a-tragedy-into-something-positive.html

Further reading/viewing

Class Dismissed: Malala's Story 2009, dir. AB Ellick, *The New York Times*. Starring Malala Yousafzai. https://www.nytimes.com/video/world/asia/100000001835296/class-dismissed-malala-yousafzais-story.html

'Following in Benazir's footsteps, Malala aspires to become PM of Pakistan', *The Express Tribune*, 10 December 2014, https://tribune.com.pk/story/804589/malala-yousafzai-17-to-receive-nobel-peace-prize/

He Named Me Malala 2015, dir. Davis Guggenheim, Fox Searchlight. Starring Malala Yousafzai.

'Malala Yousafzai made youngest UN Messenger of Peace', *BBC News*, 11 April 2017, https://www.bbc.com/news/uk-39562122

'Malala Yousafzai returns to Pakistan for first time since shooting', *BBC News*, 29 March 2018, https://www.bbc.com/news/world-asia-43578604

My Next Guest Needs No Introduction (with David Letterman) 2018, Episode 3, Netflix.

Taqi, M 2012, 'Malala and anti-Malala Pakistan', *Daily Times*, 18 October.

Thomas, R 2015, 'Malala Yousafzai: Her father's daughter', *BBC News*, 6 November.

Tohid, O 2012, 'My conversations with Malala Yousafzai, the girl who stood up to the Taliban', *Christian Science Monitor*, 11 October, https://www.csmonitor.com/World/Global-News/2012/1011/My-conversations-with-Malala-Yousafzai-the-girl-who-stood-up-to-the-Taliban

Yousafzai, M 2019, *We Are Displaced*, Weidenfeld & Nicolson, London.